STREET SMARTS

A Personal Safety Guide for Women

LOUISE RAFKIN

HarperSanFrancisco

A Division of HarperCollins*Publishers*

This book is for Ruth Samonski,
in memory of Paula Costantini.

FIRST EDITION

Library of Congress Cataloging-in-Publication Data
Rafkin, Louise
Street smarts : a personal safety guide for women / Louise Rafkin.
— 1st ed.
p. cm.
Includes bibliographical references and index.
ISBN 0–06–251211–0 (pbk. : alk paper)
1. Women—Crimes against—Prevention.   2. Self-defense for
women.
I. Title.
HV6250.4.W65R34   1995   95–18708
613.6'082–dc20   CIP

95 96 97 98 99 ❖ RRD(H) 10 9 8 7 6 5 4 3 2 1

This edition is printed on acid-free paper that meets the American
National Standards Institute Z39.48 Standard.

I WOULD LIKE TO THANK Rhoda Rafkin, Sally Randolph, and Melanie Braverman for helping with the development of this book. I would also like to acknowledge self-defense teachers Jaye Sprio and Marian van Leeuwen for offering valuable feedback on the manuscript. Most of all, I would like to thank my teacher, Barbara Niggel, for all that she has taught me, most importantly, that true strength comes from inside.

CONTENTS

CONTENTS

INTRODUCTION

YOU'RE SCARED and you should be.

Burying your head in the sand and hoping that something won't happen to you won't work. If crime hasn't happened to you, it has most likely happened to someone you know: a neighbor, relative, or coworker. Rape, robbery, assault—in the last ten years the statistics have more than doubled. The president has named the war against crime the nation's number one priority.

Unfortunately, we aren't given a large arsenal to fight this war. More people than ever are buying guns, but that hasn't slowed down the soaring crime rate. Some even claim that the proliferation of weapon-toting Americans has actually given crime a boost. Classes on personal safety are multiplying, but until self-defense is included in every school curriculum our population continues to be at risk. Meanwhile, most people glean tidbits of information about safety from talk shows, women's magazines, or office gossip.

Statistics prove that *prevention* is the most effective means of fighting crime. Becoming educated about personal safety, home security, and the nature of violent and nonviolent crime will greatly reduce your chances of being targeted for crime, theft, or personal attack.

This book will provide you with simple, sound, and well-founded advice about personal safety. As a longtime teacher of self-defense, I am commonly asked many questions—what do I do if I'm stranded in my car, how can I check on servicepeople who come to my home, how should I respond to street harassment, what should I do if faced with an armed attacker, and so on. I've included answers to these questions alongside information gleaned from police and nonbiased experts in the various fields of personal security.

Taking safety and self-defense seriously will give you more options and freedom in your life. This book will provide you with many answers to the question, How can I live more safely in this dangerous world?

CHAPTER

1

———

HOME
SAFETY

MOST CRIMES OCCUR within two miles of the home, with a huge percentage of these happening right in the home itself. Did you know it takes a burglar only two minutes to break into a house? The bulk of a burglar's time is spent looking for a building with easy access, or one that is unlocked: in nearly half of all home burglaries, access is through an open door or window. Don't take chances. Lock your doors and windows. Assess your home for safety.

Some local police offer home safety inspections. A specially trained officer will inspect your home and discuss security options. Check with your local police about this free service.

You *can* deter criminals from targeting your home.

Assessing a Neighborhood Before You Move In

- Contact the police and ask them about the crime history of the neighborhood. They may be able to tell you the specific crime history of your house or apartment.

- Visit the neighborhood several times, in the afternoon and at night. Note traffic and pedestrian patterns. This is especially important when looking for drug activity. The neighborhood might look fine during the day but come alive at night.

- Dead-end streets with little through traffic are the most safe to live on. Usually people know what cars "belong," and suspicious cars are noted. Streets with resident-only parking areas or limited parking help prevent lurkers.

- Note the parking situation. If you are using street parking, how far will you have to walk to your apartment or home? If there is a parking structure, is it isolated from the rest of the building? Is it locked? Guarded? Parking structures are frequent crime sites and are best avoided given other options.

- Are the streetlights working? Are there enough of them?

- Check for overgrown shrubbery or trees, and make sure they are trimmed back. These can be perfect hiding places for criminals.

- How far is public transportation?

- Are there twenty-four-hour or late-night stores or restaurants in the neighborhood? Check these out. They can either attract criminal activity or give you a safe haven should anything occur.

Know Your Neighborhood

Get to know your neighbors. Cultivating a sense of community and watching out for one another may be one of the best safety precautions.

- If you see suspicious people in the neighborhood, pay attention. Call the police if you think the situation merits.

- Lurking delivery or servicepeople should be reported. Check to see if they are driving company vehicles. If so, check with the company about their business in the neighborhood. If they have none, call the police.

- Note suspicious activity—people going in and out of houses at all hours, cars idling—that may indicate drug dealing, and report this to the police. Notify sympathetic neighbors and start a neighborhood watch. Log license plate numbers and other information in a journal and turn it over to the police. Ask them how you can help. Police don't want to be bothered with petty calls, but they do appreciate information.

- Make sure all public pay phones are in working order. If there is drug activity in your area, the telephone company may fix the phones so that they only work for outgoing calls. Drug dealers can't as easily do business then.

- Abandoned vehicles should be reported immediately.

Lighting

Good lighting should be well placed, and bulbs should be changed regularly. If possible, porch lights should be placed high enough so that they cannot be easily unscrewed. One woman who had recently changed the bulb in her porch light came home to find it not working. She called the police to accompany her into her home, and they caught a burglar still at work.

- Motion-activated lights are excellent deterrents.

- In apartment complexes, make sure hall, walkway, and elevator lights are working.

- Timers should be coordinated to simulate occupancy. Inexpensive timers activate single lights; the more expensive systems can program a number of appliances and lights. Some systems can vary the times day by day. Check with your hardware store or specialty safety company.

Mailboxes

Don't mark your mailbox with your name, only your street and/or apartment number. You don't want to give away personal information.

Keys

- Don't mark your keys with any identification, such as your address or phone number.

- Don't "hide" keys in obvious places or in easy-to-see locations. If necessary, use a well-hidden box with a combination lock to stash an extra key.

- Make complete copies in case of loss. Do not store these in obvious places, such as by the door. If you have trustworthy neighbors, give them an extra set of keys. Ask them to label the keys not with your name or address but with some other identifying sign.

- Color code or tag keys for quick identification to avoid fumbling with them at the door.

Doors and Door Locks

Exterior doors should be solid hardwood or steel and have strong dead bolts. Use solid locks—a dead bolt with a one-inch throw bolt or heavy-duty drop bolt is the best. Chain locks are easily broken. If you are unfamiliar with lock types, ask at a hardware store.

- You may want to put a lock on the inside of your bedroom door, especially if you have a feasible escape route through a window or second door. If you put a lock on your bedroom door, make sure the room has a phone extension.

- Always fix a faulty lock immediately.

- A lock is only as good as its strike plate. When a door is kicked in or a lock hammered, it's the strike plate holding the latch that takes the stress and often tears out of the jam. Three-inch screws that hit deep into the studs should replace the three-quarter-inch screws that come with the plates. High-security strike plates with metal screw sleeves are even better.

- Install peepholes in solid outside doors. When checking someone through a peephole at night, turn off your inside light. If you are lit from behind and someone is standing in the dark, the person can see *you* looking out.

- On outside doors, door hinge pins should be on the inside of the house. Nonremovable, hidden door pins are best.

- Dog doors can give access to long-armed intruders. Install with caution.

Windows

- Inspect all windows and add locks where necessary. Windows should be locked at all times. Keyed locking devices should be placed on double-hung windows. Make sure occupants know where keys are in case of emergency.

- Wooden rods should be placed in sliding glass doors and windows.

- A pin can be inserted in a hole drilled in the sliding-door frame to prevent anyone from lifting the door off track.

- Windows should be placed high and be free of bushes and trees.

- Burglar bars can deter break-ins, but they may also prevent firefighters from entering your home—or keep you trapped inside. Newer window grilles are equipped with quick-release features for emergency.

Alarm Systems

Criminals do not want to spend time breaking into a house. According to statistics they spend about thirty to forty-five minutes choosing their target and less than two minutes breaking in. A home with a security system is three times less likely to be broken into.

Choosing an alarm system can be tricky. Read up and don't be swayed by a smooth salesperson. When choosing a system, consider your lifestyle and other members of your household (especially children—every time anyone goes in and out the alarm must be reset). Police recommend security systems but caution against false alarms. Statistics vary, but police in one major city report that 95 percent of their house alarm calls turn out to be errors. Children, animals, strong winds, and servicepeople who don't know how to operate the system contribute to the number of false alarms. Because of the high rate of error, police are not always very quick in responding to these calls.

Costs for security systems vary from $250 for the cheapest install-it-yourself models to more than $3,000. Do-it-yourself units usually cost around $600 and offer moderate security. Dealer-installed security systems cost between $1,000 and $3,000 and provide tight, programmed security with a wide variety of features and the use of a monitoring service. When choosing a security company, ask if they are bonded and request names of satisfied clients. Ask for referrals from neighbors or police.

A one-time installation fee may not be included in your monthly service or monitoring fee. Call several companies and get quotes in writing. Keep in mind that some insurance companies will offer discounts to homeowners who install home security.

Security system tips:

- Systems are wired or wireless. A wired system has sensors placed throughout the house that are physically linked to a central control unit. In a wireless system, sensors include a small transmitter that communicates with the central control. Which system you'll use will depend a lot on whether you want to install the system yourself.

    Wireless systems are easiest to install since you are only attaching sensors to doors and windows. Wired systems require drilling holes in walls and woodwork, threading wire through walls and floors, and doing some electrical work. Wired systems are more high-end and can be less obtrusive but are usually more expensive.

    With all wired and some wireless systems, you can divide your home or apartment into zones—for example, a room, an entryway, a row of windows. Zoning helps you find and protect vulnerable areas in your home. Small houses and apartments are well suited for wireless, single-zone systems.

- Other options include "panic buttons," which you use if you are in the house and sense an intruder. These can be installed next to beds or doorways, or they can be activated by hand-held units. All systems have backup batteries to keep the system working should the power fail or a burglar attempt to disarm the system.

Outside sirens and strobe lights are another option and are recommended for single-family houses. A siren needs to reach at least eighty decibels at ten feet in order to attract attention. Often a strobe light is offered in the package, usually with wired systems. The high intensity light flashes when the siren is activated.

Professionally installed systems usually require you to subscribe to an operating service. When your alarm is tripped, an automatic dialer calls the service, and an operator calls your home. If no one answers or if a person cannot provide the code word, the operator calls the police. The cost for this service varies, and is usually billed by the year or month. Some communities will allow direct lines to the police, though in many places these are prohibited because false alarms have overloaded police switchboards.

Certain systems also include a distress option, so that if you are forced to disarm your system, it seems like you are complying but you are actually entering a code that notifies the monitoring service immediately.

- A smaller owner-operated alarm company will usually give you the most unbiased advice about your options, as opposed to a factory salesperson. In each case, find out who will install and service your alarm. According to *Consumer Reports* magazine, your chance of getting an effective security system will probably depend more on the skill and conscientiousness of your dealer than on a company's superior hardware. Read your service contract carefully; some systems are leased from the dealers, and you are only paying a rental fee.

- False security decals and signs don't fool experienced burglars. Also, the stickers that come with your alarm can reveal too much information, such as the name and model of your system. Use generic stickers or ones that don't reveal anything.

- Make sure you know how your system works—what it does and doesn't do.

- For more help choosing a security system, send for *Safe and Sound, Your Guide to Home Security* from the National Burglar and Fire Alarm Association (send $2.00 to Box 3110, Bethesda, MD 20814, or call 301-907-3202). *Consumer Reports* often runs comparisons of alarm systems. Your local librarian should be able to help you locate the most recent survey.

Dog Alarms Versus Guard Dogs

Most dog alarms sound obviously fake—barking continuously instead of stopping and starting like a real dog—and they will not deter a professional thief.

Real guard dogs can deter break-ins and are extremely effective. However, for the safety and protection of everyone, guard dogs—sometimes called command dogs—should be intelligent and well trained, not merely vicious and loud.

Elevators and Stairwells

- Don't get into an elevator with only one other person, especially if your instincts tell you not to.

- Stand next to the buttons and the door. Get out immediately if you feel unsafe.

- Don't push the stop button if you are attacked in a moving elevator. You want the car to keep moving. Push all the other buttons so the car will stop quickly. If the door opens, yell for help and try to position yourself so that the door can't close.

- Fireproof stairs block out sound. Choose your route carefully. Don't take unfamiliar stairs where doors may be locked.

Household Weapons

Formal weapons will be discussed later, but it is perhaps more important to give some thought to ordinary household items that may be used as weapons in case of an attack.

- Weapons that strike include fireplace implements, brooms, umbrellas, and garden tools. However, do not leave these outside your home where they can be picked up and used against you.

- Weapons that shield, such as a briefcase or thick scarf, can block a slashing knife. A piece of furniture, such as a chair or lamp, can block your body.

- A fire extinguisher, hairspray, or other sprays can be shot into an assailant's eyes.

- A lighted cigarette can be used to burn an attacker.

- A hot beverage can be thrown in an attacker's face.

- Keys may be used for striking or raking an assailant, especially in the vulnerable face and neck areas. Throwing keys into the face can startle an attacker and buy you some time.

Intruders

If you come home and think someone is inside, don't investigate. If you feel funny, trust yourself. Leave immediately. Go to a safe place and phone the police.

- If someone breaks in while you are at home, leave. Try to get out a window or a back exit. When calling 911 say your address first, so that if you are cut off, the police will know where to go. Teach this to your children.

- If you are asleep and wake up to a burglar already in the house, also try to leave the house safely. But if the burglar is in your room, you may want to pretend you are asleep, especially if it seems as though the person is trying to be quiet and get out before you wake. A scene may lead to your getting hurt. Your goal is to avoid confrontations with burglars.

- Make sure the intruder has a clear path of escape.

Servicepersons and Deliveries

Even if you are expecting a delivery or a serviceperson, no one should be allowed in your home without showing identification. Ask to see the identification through the peephole or a window; door chains can be easily broken. If you still feel uncomfortable or if the person is unexpected, ask for the name of the company or office—not a phone number—and call. If the person provides the number, it may be part of the setup: an accomplice may answer and back the person up. A flower delivery is an easy setup—everybody wants flowers. Check for a marked car before you open the door, or ask for the name of the flower shop and phone to verify.

If you are uncomfortable, do not allow anyone in your home. A legitimate serviceperson will understand your discomfort and arrange another appointment when you won't be alone. If it is absolutely necessary to let the serviceperson in, even after you have verified his or her identity, and you still feel uncomfortable—leave your house. Go to a neighbor's or wait in your car in front of your house until he or she is finished. Your safety is more important than your possessions, and a legitimate serviceperson will rarely steal.

Do not answer personal questions about your home life. Even a legitimate serviceperson might be setting you up for something later by asking if you live alone or if you are married. Do not lie—lying can make you more nervous. "I don't want to talk about my personal life" or

"Please, finish your job" might sound rude, but it will make you appear assertive and in control. If he or she persists or becomes angry, leave at once and notify the company and the police.

Strangers

If a stranger comes to the door, don't pretend you are not at home. You might find yourself face to face with a burglar. If you are alone, check the peephole and verify his or her identity before opening the door. If you're still unsure, talk to the person through the door.

Before answering, you might want to call out a phrase like, "John, I'll get it."

Be wary of "emergencies." If someone says he or she needs to make a call, do it for the person. Make the person wait outside while you call the police. Women are often used as fronts for this kind of break-in, because a woman is more likely to open the door to another woman. She may be working with a partner, hidden beside the house, or she may be casing your apartment for a future break-in. One woman who worked this scam had procured a mailing list from a local feminist organization. Twenty homes had been broken into before anyone connected the burglaries to the scared woman "whose purse had been snatched and who needed to call a friend." Trust your gut feelings.

Police

An estimated twenty thousand crimes a year are committed by people impersonating police officers. If the police show up at your door, ask to see identification and a shield before opening your door. Still, these items are relatively easy to obtain. Don't hesitate to call their precinct or department to verify their identity before letting them inside.

Telephone Safety

Don't answer phone surveys. They are nearly always scams to get you to buy something or to get personal information about your housing situation—for example, "How many people live in your house?" or "Are you married?"

Don't reveal "numbers" over the phone. A con artist might ask for information to verify a contest prize, or someone may impersonate a bank officer in order to get information about your accounts. Don't give your credit card, Social Security card, or phone card numbers. Never give bank account or personal identification numbers (PIN) over the phone.

Don't leave your name or personal information on your answering machine message, and never leave information about travel plans. "This is 555-1212. Please leave a message" is boring but most safe. Use "we" in your message even if you live alone.

Phone Harassment

What to do about harassing phone calls:

- Keep a record of hang-ups and annoying or harassing calls. After the second call, report details to the police. The police will work with the telephone company, and they will notify you when they have traced more information. Most phone companies have an Annoyance Call Bureau listed in the phone book.

- Harassing phone calls may not feel dangerous, yet they may escalate into a situation that is threatening to your safety. A stalker may begin by harassing you over the phone; a thief or rapist might assess your reaction to intimidation by assessing your response to either a silent or obscene call. Say, "I am calling the police," then hang up immediately.

- If you use an answering machine, change your message to say that your phone is being tapped by the telephone company.

- People who make obscene phone calls most often just want to annoy you. Don't engage them. Press the switch hook and say, "Operator, I would like this call traced." Then hang up immediately.

- If you know who is calling, inquire about the availability of call blocking in your area. For a small monthly fee, this service allows you to reject calls from selected numbers.

PHONE CALLER IDENTIFICATION SERVICES

Available in many areas, caller identification allows you to screen calls and identify the source of harassing phone calls. A caller identification machine attaches to your phone and displays the number of an incoming call. These machines are available with a variety of options and run from $25 to $300. The more expensive machines record your last twenty to eighty calls.

Before buying a caller identification machine, contact your local phone company to find out if caller identification is available in your area. This service, for which there is a monthly fee, must first be activated by the phone company in order for any caller ID unit to work. At the moment, phone companies can relay numbers only, but name transmission will be available in the near future.

However, caller identification machines can be thwarted by "line blocking" or "per-call blocking." Line blocking is done through the phone company and prevents a person's number from appearing on anyone's caller identification machine. Per-call blocking is done by pushing a set number before dialing.

In spite of this complicated new service, the best way to treat harassing phone calls is to notify the police and the phone company's annoyance bureau. Most phone companies now have codes for helping you trace and track obscene or harassing calls. If you have a police complaint number, the phone company will begin a file of your traced calls and notify you about how to follow up with the police.

Possessions

- Make an inventory of your possessions, and keep it current.

- Don't keep valuables in obvious places. Expensive or sentimentally valuable jewelry should be creatively hidden, not placed in a jewelry box on a bathroom or bedroom counter. Money and documents should also be stored in unobtrusive places.

- There are a number of "fake" safes on the market. Designed to look like video cassettes, cans of cleanser, books, or food products, these are not actually locked safes but camouflaged hiding places for valuables.

- Always remember to place personal safety before the safety of possessions.

CHAPTER 2

STREET SURVIVAL

BEING SAFE ON THE STREET and in your day-to-day life requires awareness. Keep in mind that attackers and criminals are looking for easy targets, people who are easy to intimidate and control.

Have a Plan

With a friend, walk your neighborhood and other frequent haunts. Note the location of public telephones and all-night stores. Note back alleys—where do they lead? Are there any escape routes you could use if forced into a corner? Talk with your friend about strategies you might use in various situations.

Even when walking in unfamiliar areas, try to plan ahead. Consult a map, and consider driving through the area first. Try to find a person who knows the area and ask them for information.

Posture and Attitude

Victim selection is usually made within the first thirty seconds of an encounter. Act confident even if you are scared. Keep your head up, and breathe. Breathing will calm you as well as provide air if you need to run or yell.

- Walk assertively: head up and shoulders back. Stay aware; scan your path. Appear alert but disinterested. Practice this look in shop windows and your bathroom mirror. Watch how others carry themselves on the street. Do they appear vulnerable or assertive?

- Walk well away from recessed doorways or shop entrances. Walk in the middle of the sidewalk against traffic to deter purse snatchers or attacks from behind.

- Keep at least one arm free; don't load yourself down with packages.

- Don't use headphones on the street. You are cut off from your surroundings and can be easily surprised.

- Make brief eye contact as you walk. Don't look away if you are being studied. Make sure they know you know they are there.

- Ideally, keep a two-arms' distance between you and others.

The "Don't Mess with Me" Look

Attackers will target vulnerable people. If you are being cased, use nonverbal defense to indicate you are not scared or intimidated.

- Set your face; make it appear serious and strong.

- Make eye contact—don't look down. Looking down shows you are intimidated. When making eye contact, don't give off a friendly or open look. Squinting the eyes slightly helps counter this. If you are being stared at, give a good, strong look and then glance away—not down. Then give your "don't mess with me" look again and let the person know you are not intimidated. You don't want the situation to escalate; you want to appear strong and confident.

- Develop your own strong, confident look and practice this in the mirror. Practice while walking down the street. Glance at yourself in a shop window. Do you look vulnerable or confident?

Street-smart Dressing

Women are often wrongly told that they "asked" for trouble by dressing certain ways. But although sexy or so-called provocative dressing does not invite attack, there are things to consider when dressing for successful self-defense.

- Wear sunglasses if you are hesitant to make eye contact—they allow you to see others without being seen.

- Wear shoes that you can move in—or quickly lose.

- If you are pushed to the ground, forget your modesty. One street mugger said he targeted women in skirts because they fussed with their clothing rather than fighting him off.

- If you are going to wear expensive jewelry, carry it until you reach your destination—especially if you are taking public transportation or walking a distance from your car.

Purses, Bags, and Backpacks

- Before your leave home, remove things you won't need that day: driver's license if you won't be driving, all but one credit card and check if you won't be shopping. The less you carry, the less hesitant you will be to give up your bag.

- Shoulder bags should be carried toward the front of the body, not bouncing against your back. Most safe: Carry it over a shoulder and tucked under an arm like a football. In cold weather, strap your purse across your body but under your overcoat. If you strap your purse across your body on the outside of your clothing, you may be hurt if someone grabs and pulls.

- Backpacks with back pockets are easy targets for thieves, especially in crowded subways or buses. Take the pack off when stationary or in a group of people.

- Carry your real valuables—keys, wallet—in pockets.

Street Harassment

- Wolf whistles and street harassment by men—staring, comments on your body or dress—are best countered with nonverbal responses. Look directly at the offender and let him know you know he is there. Look strong, head high and steady. Make him know you are not easily intimidated. He may be trying to assess how vulnerable you are and possibly target you for attack.

- Educating, or holding the harasser accountable for his remarks, may seem tempting, but your primary goal is to stay safe. Don't fire back obscenities or threats, as they are likely to escalate the situation into something more intense or violent. You don't want to irritate the offender into taking physical action against you.

- Continue with head up, walking confidently.

- Be aware of the distance between you and the harasser. Glance behind you until he is well out of range—more than three-arms' distance.

If You Are Being Followed

On a busy street:

- Cross the street and go in the other direction. Or, wait for the person to pass so that *you* are the one following. Let the person know you know. Next, go for help, if needed. If there are others around, call attention to your situation: "Stop following me. Leave me alone!"

- Walk up to someone and start to speak as if with an acquaintance. Talking with a shopkeeper or street vender might dissuade the person following from engaging with you.

On a deserted street:

- Go for help. Assess who is around and how far it is to help. Are there storefront windows (preferably with alarms) that could be broken? What can you do to make a scene and alert others? If no one is around, prepare to confront the attacker while increasing your awareness. (See chapter 7, "Physical Self-defense," especially the section on verbal self-defense.)

- Don't lead an attacker to your home, especially if no one is home. You are safer on the street than you would be in your home or in an elevator. If you go home, the person following knows where you can be found later.

- If someone comes up behind you just as you approach your home, do not go inside if it is empty unless no other option is available. You don't want someone following you inside.

- If someone is at home, or there are neighbors nearby who might hear you, ring the doorbell or knock loudly. Call attention to the situation and yell out, "Call the police!" The possibility of the police or other help arriving may deter the attacker.

- If you cannot attract attention, turn and face the attacker at the door and immediately use your voice. Be prepared to use physical defense, and scan the area for possible escape routes. You may also choose to turn and strike first if you feel the threat of physical harm is imminent.

Drawing Attention

Drawing attention on the street or in a public place can bring help and discourage an attacker from pursuing you. Getting over the fear of making a scene is crucial, but don't count on other people helping.

- State the obvious. "That man is bothering me" may work if someone is staring or otherwise harassing you. "You are standing too close, move back." Other people will notice.

- Break a window by throwing something or by swinging your purse or briefcase. A shattering window will attract attention, especially if it is wired to a burglar alarm. Remember, property is easily replaced, your well-being is not.

Homeless Persons, Panhandlers, and People Under the Influence

Most people who live on the streets are not violent criminals and are not a threat to your safety. However, people under the influence of alcohol or drugs *can* act erratically.

- If you feel unsafe, trust your gut. Cross the street. Avoid the situation altogether.

- If you feel uncomfortable with panhandlers, simply keep walking with full awareness.

- If you give money, don't flash a full wallet. Other people may be watching.

- Don't engage with people under the influence of alcohol or drugs. Avoid eye contact and leave at once.

Angry Strangers

If you encounter an angry or out-of-control stranger, leave at once. Cross the street. Run away. You never know if the person will pull a weapon or strike out violently. Don't be there. If you witness a scene—an angry person in a restaurant or office building—don't stick around for the show.

- Don't try to find out what is wrong or try to fix it. An angry person will not be able to hear reason or take advice. Don't engage.

- If someone yells something at you from a car, don't yell back.

- If you need to engage with the person—say you *did* scratch his or her car—you must de-escalate the situation. "Calm down and I'll talk to you. Calm down." This must be said in a firm but not angry or threatening way. Be assertive. Assure the person you can hear him or her. "Calm down. I'll get the police." Keep repeating the command "calm down" until you feel safe enough to either get help or have a reasonable conversation.

- Keep a two-arms' distance between you and the angry person at all times.

- Don't engage in swearing or name-calling. They will only escalate the situation.

Strangers with Questions

An unbelievable ten thousand crimes each year begin with someone asking for directions or the time. Though it may seem impolite, don't engage with strangers. If you choose to give the time, don't engage further. Say, "I can't help you," and if you know where help can be found, you might add, "The police station (or service station) is up there on the right."

Asking directions is a great way to glean personal information. Many people asking directions start with the question, "Are you from around here?" Already, by answering you are telling personal information, letting the attacker know whether you are in familiar territory or if you are a tourist. If you give directions, never go up to a car window, and never call someone to your own car window.

Avoiding Friendliness

Many people feel compelled to return smiles and greetings on the street. We are taught to be polite and friendly. Sometimes this can get us into trouble. A friendly smile on the street can turn into a leer. Idle chat with a friendly service station attendant can quickly turn uncomfortable if he steers talk toward your personal life. Chitchat on a bus can lead to someone insisting on walking you home. Remember, attackers are looking for easy targets. Your open, friendly manner makes their work easy.

- Practice *not* being polite. Notice how often you smile at someone you don't know or don't feel comfortable with.

- On the street, don't feel compelled to return greetings from strangers. Nodding acknowledges the greeting without opening yourself up. Keep walking.

If a polite conversation veers into uncomfortable territory:

- Stand your ground. If you feel that the situation is fairly safe, say, "I don't want to talk about my personal life," or "I'm not comfortable talking about this with you."

- If you feel threatened, unsafe, or that the conversation is out of bounds, say, "Stop. I don't want to talk with you. Leave me alone." If the person doesn't leave, you leave.

- Report inappropriate behavior by servicepeople to company superiors. A gas company employee was fired after several women reported him prying into their living situations. "Are these your kids?" in reference to pictures on a refrigerator can quickly lead to "Are you married?" or "Does your husband work?" All too soon, your personal safety may be threatened.

Pickpockets

Pickpockets usually work in teams. Be alert to people bumping you, touching you in any way, or falling in front of you. As you help the stumbling man up, he may be helping himself. Guard your wallet, and don't count or display your money in public.

ATM Safety

- As much as possible, use well-lit, busy ATMs in well-populated locations during daylight hours. Be aware of your surroundings and look around frequently.

- ATMs with counter keyboards are more private—others cannot easily see your identification number. With the older machines, use your body to block the screen when entering your code.

- Choose drive-up ATMs over walk-ups. Keep your car running.

- Avoid ATMs that are surrounded by shrubbery or trees, and don't use ATMs at the rear entrances of buildings or banks.

- Put away your money immediately. Don't count it at the machine or sit in a parked car next to an ATM.

- Always take your transaction slip.

- Notify your bank as soon as your card is missing or stolen. If you do this within two days, your liability is limited to $50; after two days the loss limit is $500.

- Cooperate with an armed robber. If you are approached, stay calm by breathing deeply. Tell the robber he or she can have your money. "Anything you want, just don't hurt me" is a good statement. Give up the money—hand it over or throw it on the ground away from the door—and leave as soon as possible. Contact the police immediately. Do not go *anywhere* with the robber. If you are asked to withdraw more money, do so. You will only be responsible for $50 of the withdrawal.

- Pilot programs are revising ATMs to make them safer. At several test sites, emergency phone buttons have been installed that are connected with the police.

Tips for Runners and Athletes

- Don't wear earphones—you can't hear what's going on around you, and you tend to lose track of who's nearby. (Sorry!)

- Exercise in prime time—before or after work, when others are out.

- Try to avoid secluded, bushy, or tree-lined paths where an assailant could hide. If possible, before going on foot, drive your proposed route to survey the area. Make note of twenty-four-hour stores, phone boxes, and possible escape routes.

- A dog is a good running companion.

- Ignore comments and verbal harassment. Keep moving.

- If you think a car is following you, turn around. Run the other way. If the car persists, quickly go to a public place—a store or an apartment with a guard—and yell, "Fire! Help! I'm being followed," to attract attention.

- Keep identification somewhere on your body. Write the name of a contact person and any pertinent medical information. This can be life-saving should you need assistance.

Safety on Public Transportation

- Try to arrive just minutes before departure. This prevents you from hanging out and being studied as a target.

- Don't sit alone. On buses, sit behind the driver or with others. As you arrive at your destination, scan the stop for anyone lurking. If you spot someone suspicious or feel apprehensive, stay on board or ask the driver to wait a few moments.

- Don't sit in train cars with people who make you uncomfortable. Avoid gangs of friends, drunks, or sports fans. Find another car immediately.

- Use well-lighted stops.

- Keep at least one hand free when carrying packages.

- Don't sleep. Stay alert!

- If someone hassles you, don't ignore it. Use your voice loudly. Call attention to your situation. If the person persists, hit the emergency device. Don't leave the car for an empty platform or station. Make sure there is help available before getting off the train.

- If a man is rubbing against you or otherwise touching you inappropriately, make him publicly accountable for his actions and let him know you aren't easily intimidated. "Stop touching me" or "Move back" said in a calm, loud, and confident voice will bring attention to the situation.

Safety in Taxis

- If you feel uncomfortable getting into a taxi, trust your gut and flag another.

- Note the taxi company and the driver's name and number. If something feels strange, tell the driver to stop. Mention the driver's name so the person knows you have noted his or her identity.

CHAPTER

3

——

TRAVEL
SAFETY

VACATIONERS TEND TO RELAX, sometimes a bit too much. Sound self-defense skills work in any venue, yet there are additional factors to consider, especially if you are traveling to foreign countries. Talking to others who are familiar with your destination will help you prepare. Also, watch for cultural red flags. For example, in some countries men are more verbally aggressive on the street. Though the threat of violence in such countries may not be as high as it is elsewhere, it is important to be aware so you won't be caught off guard.

Standards of dress for women may differ in foreign countries. Familiarize yourself with local customs by reading or by talking with travel agents. This way, you may be less noticeable and more comfortable while traveling.

Luggage and Valuables

- Fanny packs and belt bags advertise important contents. Carry valuables in more hidden places, such as under-the-arm shoulder holsters or money belts.

- Distraction thieves may work in teams for clever pickpocketing. Be careful of people asking for directions, "tripping" in front of you (especially with someone else coming to the person's rescue), or spilling something on you that they then offer to wipe off. These are all common airport theft ploys.

- Watch your carry-on luggage through the X-ray machine—if you are stopped at the machine yourself, make sure your bags are safe at the end of the conveyer belt, or ask to set them next to the metal detector so you can see them.

- Lock luggage. For extra protection against theft, wrap bags with electrical tape. Theft by airport employees has been on the rise.

- Luggage tags should be face down in their sleeves.

Rental Cars

- Do not rent a car that displays the name of the rental company. If the car is marked with the company name, request an "unmarked" car.

- Don't leave anything of value in your car, and be wary of using maps at intersections; a carjacker hanging out at the corner will target you as an easy mark and ask if you need directions.

- Track your route to your destination before leaving the airport. Some companies offer a computerized printout with directions from the airport to your destination.

- Most rental companies in major cities rent portable cellular phones—great for emergencies or a hook-up to police. These usually cost under $10 a day with an added per-call charge.

Choosing a Safe Hotel

When traveling, call ahead to pick a hotel with good security.

- Ask about twenty-four-hour desk staffing and about room phones.

- Pick a hotel with doors that open to the inside of the building, not to a balcony, walkway, or parking lot. You don't want to be observed.

- Ask about door keys. The best are the electronic strip cards, which are reprogrammed after every guest. Keys with the name and room number of the hotel are the worst.

- Self-locking dead bolts are best. Peepholes help to identify room service personnel.

Hotel Safety

- When checking in, ask that your room number be written down rather than announced for all to hear. Don't repeat the number to verify. Have a hotel bellhop accompany you into your room to make sure no one is inside.

- Use all locks and chains all the time.

- Criminals may impersonate hotel personnel. If you order room service, ask for the bill to be slipped under the door before you open it.

- Verify any unexpected deliveries or maintenance requests by calling the front desk and/or maintenance departments.

- Use the hotel safe for money and valuables.

- Don't leave your telephone calling card visible when you go out.

- If you don't need your room straightened, leave a "do not disturb" sign on the door. The most common hotel crime is theft.

While Away

- Stop newspaper and mail delivery.

- Alert neighbors to your travel plans.

- Install at least two timed lights, including a porch light. Don't leave lights on all night—it's a clear sign that you are gone.

- Radios can be set on timers and are good deterrents.

- Arrange for yard and lawn care if you are going for an extended time.

CHAPTER

4

CAR
SAFETY

MOST OF US SPEND so much time in our cars it's no wonder crimes involving cars are such a worry. There are simple ways to protect yourself in and around your vehicle.

Going to Your Car

- Approach your car with your keys in hand. Scan the area around the car as you get closer, and glance under the car to see that no one is hiding.

- Be aware of people approaching you, asking directions, handing out fliers—in general of anyone getting too close to you as you get into your car. Keep at least two-arms' distance away from them.

- Check the interior of the car before opening the door. Make this a habit.

- If you've been shopping with children, load your packages in the car before you put the kids inside. If your car gets carjacked, your family will still be safe with you.

On the Road

The most important thing is to plan ahead: know where you are going and check a map.

- Always keep your doors locked and the windows at least part-way up.

- Hide all packages, purses, and personal items under the driver's seat.

- When stopping at lights or stop signs, try to leave enough room around your car to maneuver so that you are not totally pinned in.

- In city driving, use the centermost lane.

- Don't stop to help someone who is broken down. Drive to a safe phone and call the police.

Harassment While Driving

If someone is making gestures, trying to make eye contact, or otherwise harassing you from within another car, give the person a firm, no-nonsense, leave-me-alone stare and continue driving. Don't escalate being hassled into a potentially dangerous situation by yelling, swearing, or returning the gesture. Drive away or keep clear if you are still traveling the same road. You never know when someone can snap and become violent, or who may be carrying a weapon.

Parking Safety

Always try to park in well-lit, high-traffic locations. Park near the entrances of malls or shopping areas, especially if you are going to leave your car unattended for any length of time. Avoid parking next to dumpsters or wooded areas with limited visibility. At night, find a well-lit area.

- People should not be hanging out in parking lots. Report anyone who seems to be casing your car to parking attendants, police, or security. If you are scared to return to your car—because people are hanging around—call the police or a security guard for an escort.

- Don't park next to vans or trucks. Someone may be lurking inside, waiting to pull you in.

- Especially when parking in structures, be sure to find a spot near a public walkway or elevator. Wait for other people—preferably several groups—before you leave your vehicle.

- When using valet parking, leave only your car key.

- When parking in ticketed parking structures, take your slip with you—don't leave it on your dash in plain view. Without a ticket, a car thief would have to pay the maximum amount to get your car out. Perhaps the person will steal something cheaper.

Getting Lost and Asking Directions

Your best option is to go to the police, if you can figure out where they might be. (This is where a car phone comes in very handy.) If you can't find the police, ask for directions at a service station, or ask a store owner, but try not to ask in front of other people. You don't want others to know you are unfamiliar with the area and therefore vulnerable. Do not call to someone on the street to come to your car window. People may tell you wrong directions and follow you to a secluded area.

Breakdowns

- Pull over and put on your flashers. If you have a "Call Police" sunshield, put it in the back window. Do not get out of your car. Wait for the police.

- If a man stops, crack your window and ask him to call the police or a tow truck. Even if the helpful person is a woman, be careful. She may have an accomplice hiding.

- You can pass money for a call through the window, but don't roll the window down.

- If you stock your car with water, a blanket, flares, and even dry food (especially if you have children), breaking down will be less stressful.

Accidents

If you get involved in a fender bender, motion the driver to follow you to the nearest gas or police station. Once you have pulled over, keep your windows and doors locked until someone else, preferably the police, has arrived. Keep the engine running. Ask for insurance information to be passed through the window and demand that someone call the police. Note the license number of the car. When help arrives you may get out of your car, but don't leave valuables behind.

If you are in an accident and your car is disabled, you may choose to stay in the car until help has arrived. Be sure there is no danger of explosion.

Being Pulled Over

Don't assume that anyone with a uniform and flashing light is a cop. It is easy to purchase police uniforms and badges. If you are flashed, first ask yourself if you have broken the law.

Check the car: Is it marked with identifiable police markings? Be wary of unmarked cars and plainclothes police officers, as police rarely use unmarked cars for traffic violations. You have the right to request a uniformed police officer before you get out of your car.

Once you have pulled over, keep your door locked. Check the police car and the identification of the officer before cracking your window and sliding out your license. Try to pull over in well-populated and well-lighted areas. If need be, flip your turn signal or emergency lights on and make a sign that you are cooperating but driving to a safer place. Most patrol persons will understand not wanting to stop in an isolated area.

If You Are Being Followed in Your Car

If you are being followed, do not drive home. Go to a police or fire station, a hospital emergency room, or another well-lit and populated area. If the pursuer persists, lay on the horn when you stop and keep your doors locked.

If you think the person following you may be angry and/or violent, do not stop the car until there is help. Keep driving and try to attract and signal the police. Several women have been killed by abusive partners who have followed them in order to "talk." Remember, talking to an angry or violent person only increases the potential for violence. Your safety comes first.

Carjacking

Although the media has stirred up quite a lot of hype about carjackings, statistically your chances of being a victim of this crime are pretty low. However, in some places the risk is real and growing. The rise in carjacking may be due to the increased numbers of car alarms (making it as easy to steal an occupied car as a parked car) or the high resale value of stolen cars. Whatever the reasons, there are ways to deter carjackers and deal with the situation should it occur.

- If you are outside your car and face a carjacker with a weapon, assure the attacker you will give up your car. Say, "Okay, here are my keys." Don't argue or resist. Drop your keys on the ground near the attacker and run in the other direction. If you have another set of keys on you—post office keys, unmarked office keys—*and* if there is help nearby, throw those while you run to safety. By the time the carjacker figures out they aren't the right keys you will be safe.

- If you are in your car with the windows rolled up, you may choose to drive away, especially if you have a clear escape route. Even carjackers with guns probably won't break a window with a gun, and they probably won't shoot if you drive away.

- If you witness a carjacking or attempted carjacking, note the license number and call the police. As you leave the crime site yell, "I'm calling the police!"

- *A cellular car phone is an excellent safety tool.* If you have to call for help, you have it right there.

Abduction Attempts

If you are approached by a man with a weapon and told to go with him in your car, or in his, *don't*. You may be told that if you go, you won't be hurt—but don't believe what an attacker says.

Don't negotiate. Remember, you are dealing with someone who is committing a crime and is not likely to keep his word. If there are threats, remember this: You are less likely to get hurt if you get out of the situation without getting in the car with the attacker. Going to what the police call a "secondary crime site" is one of the most dangerous moves you can make. Instead, you should run. The odds of getting shot in the back running away are less than the odds of being killed if you go with the assailant, giving him time to think about what he will do to you, when, where, and how.

Even if you are fired at from behind, the odds of getting fatally wounded are slight, certainly less than those of people who accompany a criminal to a secondary crime site. Figures show that over 85 percent of the people who go to secondary crime sites are seriously injured.

- If someone reaches into your window, be creative. Quickly roll up the window, or bend back the person's fingers. A handy cigarette lighter can burn an attacker's hand and cause a hasty retreat.

- If someone forces their way into your car, escape as soon as possible. If you can leave your car, do so. Jump out at a red light and run.

- If you are forced to go in your car with the attacker, consider crashing the car or causing an accident. (One that won't injure you severely: for example, driving onto a lawn.) After a crash or an accident, jump out and run.

Preventing Theft

A car is stolen every nineteen seconds. Nearly 15 percent of stolen cars were left unlocked. Lock your car, everywhere. Especially at home. When parking, turn your wheels to the curb or sideways. Ten percent of stolen cars are towed away.

Engraving the car's vehicle inspection number (VIN) on the windshield and other body parts may deter a thief who is hoping for quick resale.

Consider buying some kind of antitheft device. Check with your insurance company—many give discounts of up to 30 percent to drivers who equip their cars with antitheft devices.

- Alarms. The market is flooded with all kinds of alarms. The best way to pick an alarm is to go to an auto-alarm store (not a car dealer) and discuss your options. Some alarms are activated by locking the door. These are preferred by insurance companies over those activated by a hand-held device. The siren should be loud enough to attract attention and should include a cut-off time (about three minutes) so you won't irritate those nearby during the inevitable false alarms.

- Steering wheel/brake combination locks can be bought for about $50.

- A steel or alloy steering-column cover will block access to the ignition, and they cost between $85 and $150.

- Steering-wheel bar locks are good deterrents. Although the steel bars can be cut by a professional, these locks, which prevent car wheels from turning more than a few degrees, will deter amateurs. The Club, the most popular of these devices, will reimburse $500 toward your insurance deductible if your car is stolen while equipped with their product. Bar locks cost about $60.

- Kill switches that shut down the fuel system can be installed by a mechanic and are quite effective. They won't stop someone from breaking in or stealing the car, but they will stop the thief from driving away. Several of these devices disable the starter motor and prevent the car from turning over. Costs vary, from $200 to $1,000.

- Tracking systems that enable police to locate a vehicle are also effective, but they are more expensive and not available in all areas. Also, a smart thief can drive your car out of tracking range within a few hours. They cost between $600 and $1,500, plus a monthly fee of about $20.

If your car is missing, first call the police. Find out if it has only been towed or is actually stolen. Next, call your insurance company.

Record the pertinent information about your car and keep this information somewhere other than in your car. Note the license plate, vehicle identification, and serial numbers. If your car is stolen, the police will enter this data into the National Crime Information Computer, which makes your car traceable nationwide.

Car Registration

Unless you use a post office box for your car registration, black out your address before stashing the registration in your glove compartment. Parking attendants or car thieves can get your address and burglarize your home. (Police computers can now prove ownership and verify your address even if you don't have the registration with you.)

Automatic Garage Door Openers

With your address and your garage door opener, a thief can drive right in. Hide your garage door opener, don't just store it in the glove box. Better still, carry it in your purse or bag.

CHAPTER 5

SOCIAL, INTIMATE, AND WORK RELATIONSHIPS

MORE PEOPLE ARE TARGETED for crimes and violence by people they know or by their acquaintances than they are by strangers. Setting limits with people you know is often more difficult than dealing with strangers. The difference between what is dangerous and what is bothersome is more difficult to assess with people who are familiar, or in intimate relationships and friendships. Practice and awareness are the keys to keeping your personal, professional, and social relationships healthy and safe.

Boundaries in the Workplace

According to recent government statistics, women have a one-in-four chance of being assaulted, harassed, or threatened at work. Staying safe at work involves awareness. Though there are considerations to be made if you are dealing with a boss, co-worker, or the public, it is always important to be aware of both your safety and your personal boundaries. You have a right to feel safe and secure in your workplace. Here is some general advice about workplace boundaries.

- Don't engage in conversations that make you uncomfortable. Excuse yourself and walk away, or say, "I'm not comfortable discussing this."

- Comments about clothing or appearance should be offered professionally, without sexual suggestion or innuendo. If these comments seem out of place or awkward, say, "I'm not comfortable with your comments about my appearance. I would prefer that you keep your opinions to yourself." You don't have to be rude; be firm and confident.

- You are not under obligation to reveal anything about your personal life, marital status, or sexual preference to employers or potential employers. If asked, say you would prefer to keep your personal life private.

- Walk away from sexual joking or offensive comments among co-workers. Say you are uncomfortable with the conversation.

- If you find yourself questioning someone's behavior toward you, talk to a trusted friend or coworker. Usually harassers are targeting more than one person, and you might find others in your situation. You can then choose to make a plan regarding reporting the offense or filing a complaint.

Sexual Harassment

Sexual harassment is not about sex, but about power. It is also illegal. Sexual harassment is defined as any unwelcome sexual contact that is a term or condition of employment or that creates an intimidating, hostile, or offensive work environment. A harasser can be an employer, workmate, employee, or nonemployee (client or vendor).

Sexual harassment can be verbal or physical. If you have experienced any of the following at work it may be sexual harassment:

- Suggestive comments about your body or appearance

- Sexual advances

- Unwanted touching

- Exposure to pornography

If you think you are being harassed, trust your instincts. Then:

- Clearly tell the offender to stop. First do so verbally.

- Start a record of the offensive behavior. Note the date, time, and specifics of every situation. Keep a copy of this document at home.

- Tell a third party. Let someone else know the problem exists. Look for witnesses or other victims.

- Inform the harasser in writing about the offensive behavior.

If you need help drafting a letter or setting a course of action, contact an attorney, your union chair, or a legal aid center. Some companies have grievance procedures for employees. There are several good books available about the rights of victims of sexual harassment, including *Sexual Harassment on the Job: What It Is and How to Stop It* by attorneys William Petrocelli and Barbara Kate Repa (1992, Nolo Press, 950 Parker Street, Berkeley, CA 94710). *The Nine to Five Guide to Combatting Sexual Harassment: Candid Advice from 9 to 5, the National Association of Working Women* by Ellen Bravo and Ellen Cassedy (1992, John Wiley & Sons, 605 Third Avenue, New York, NY 10158) is also a good resource. The organization *9 to 5* runs a national hotline at (800) 522-0925. If you are being harassed, call for free advice.

A note about legal action: Under new laws, victims of sexual harassment may sue for damages for pain and suffering as well as for lost pay. You may also recover legal fees.

Working Late or Shift Work

The most important thing when working late is to make sure *someone* knows where you are—call a friend or, if it's a secured building, notify security. If it's a regular late shift, make sure at least one person knows your work schedule, or knows where to find a copy of it. That way, if you are missing or don't turn up when expected, someone knows when you last worked.

- Keep the number for building security handy, even if you've called to let them know you'll be working late.

- If possible, lock your office door. Try not to be the only person in the building.

- Keep lights on around your work station.

- Check all exits and entrances to make sure they are securely locked.

- If you have a choice, try not to work late in an area that can be viewed from the outside.

Violence in the Workplace

High-stress jobs create the potential for violence. Social work, government work, or any situation where a possibly angry public has access to you can be dangerous. Numbers of workplace crimes and murders have doubled in the last ten years. As more of these crimes hit the news, mass murders and violent crime by disgruntled members of the public or by one's co-workers have given cause for concern.

- Watch for signs of unusual behavior in co-workers that might lead to obsession or violence. The profile of a workplace offender is someone who is depressed, shows erratic behavior or mood swings, or is paranoid, sullen or given to tantrums. He might also have an interest in collecting weapons. Trust your gut feelings. Report the behavior and get help if you feel there is a threat of violence.

- Monitor your workspace. Be aware of people who appear agitated. Don't ignore your gut feelings.

- Make sure your company and coworkers have plans for dealing with violent or erratic behavior. Several workplace murders have occurred even though the victim reported the harasser's behavior and threats to superiors. The superiors did not act on the complaints. Be persistent and follow up on your complaints.

- Make sure you have clear avenues of escape at your desk. If your cubicle or office is big enough, arrange your office furniture so that a harasser in front of your desk will not block the doorway.

- Don't try to reason with angry people. Try saying, "Calm down and I'll talk with you" three times. If they persist, suggest they return another time. If they don't leave at this point, get help. Phone for help, or if you think you are in danger, leave. If you must leave your office space, alert your coworkers and call security and/or the police.

- Don't be a hero. Your safety is more important than taming a wild customer, co-worker, or disgruntled member of the public. If you must leave the building entirely, do so. Leave as soon as you feel a threat of violence, even though this may seem premature. If there is violence to property, leave immediately. Making a decision to leave your workplace may involve some explanation later, especially if the harasser is a boss, co-worker, or superior. But it is important to take action in order to keep yourself safe.

- If an incident is occurring elsewhere in the workplace, don't investigate. Get yourself to safety or, if necessary, hide. Try to alert security or the police, but get to safety first.

Personal Information

The less information available about you the better. In a variety of seemingly innocent situations, stalkers and other criminals may be assessing you, gathering information about your life and routines. Here are additional tips for keeping your life private and more safe:

- Get a personal mailbox at a private mail drop. This is safer than using a U.S. post box.

- Checks should be marked with your first initial and last name, your post office box and address, but *not* your phone number. You are not required to provide your phone number. If you are asked by a shop clerk for your number, you can always give a false one. Remember, you may not have to worry about the clerk, but what about the guy behind you in line. . . .

- Don't give out your home address or phone number on computer bulletin boards—you have no way of verifying a person's identity.

- Warn children not to give personal information about their parents or their whereabouts to questioning strangers.

- In a majority of states, anyone can get your telephone number and address from the Department of Motor Vehicles by making a request and paying a small fee. This availability is being contested in government hearings, but opposition from mail-marketing firms, the press, and private investigators is jamming up the push for change. Get a post office box and change the address on your license. Do not provide your phone number.

- Don't list your home address and phone on contest entries, drawings, or petitions. These may be copied by anyone.

- Monitor what kind of meeting information you list in church, community, or school bulletins. One widows' group listed their monthly meeting place in a church bulletin. Burglars targeted the previous weeks' hostesses for some time before anyone caught on to the scheme.

Rape

Power, anger, and control are the motives for rape—not sex. Therefore, a strong, assertive, self-confident person is less likely to be targeted for attack. However, no one is to be blamed for being attacked, and no one is immune from attack. Nearly 700,000 American women are raped each year, and nearly one in eight women will be the target of a forcible sexual assault in their lifetime.

There are no right and wrong ways to handle a rape attempt. It depends on the situation, the attacker, and your environment. Surviving is the goal. Statistics show that fighting off an attacker—screaming, hitting, or running—improves your chances of fending off a rape without making you more vulnerable to other injury.

- Assess your situation. How close is help? Is there a weapon involved? Breathe to calm yourself.

- Pleading and crying will usually worsen the situation.

- If possible, try to escape. Do not get into a car with an attacker *unless not to do so would cause you severe injury.* Scream. Run. Quickly. You are less likely to be injured while escaping than if you go with an attacker to what the police call a "secondary crime site." Of the people who go with armed attackers in a vehicle escape, 88 percent receive *serious* injury. An attacker with a gun is not likely to shoot you in the back if you run, *especially* if you are in a populated area.

- Fight back with conviction. See chapter 7, "Physical Self-defense."

- If you are attacked in your home, get out and get help. Chances are it will be harder to make the attacker leave your home than to leave yourself. Scream "Help! Fire!" and run to a neighbor's house or a public place. If you are partially clothed, do not wait to dress to leave the house. Though you may be embarrassed, an attempted rape is not your fault.

- In a date-rape situation, make what is happening very clear. Even if you are making out or have been sexually intimate before, sex against your will is rape. Use the word "rape." Say, "Stop. You are raping me," rather than, "Stop! I don't like this." Bring reality into the picture.

If you are raped:

- Get to a safe place.

- Call a rape crisis center, local hospital, or the police. The National Victim Center, (800) FYI-CALL, will refer you to the nearest rape crisis center. Reporting rape can be an empowering experience.

- Don't take a shower or comb your hair.

- Keep the clothes worn at the time of the attack for medical and forensic exam.

- Get a medical exam.

If you are raped, remember: Nothing you did was wrong. Victims of acquaintance rape often blame themselves for not having "known better." You are not at fault.

Dating Strategies and New Acquaintances

National statistics show that nearly 85 percent of all rapes are committed by acquaintances—attackers who know or recognize their victims. This can be a family member, acquaintance, or date. With careful planning, nonverbal and verbal self-defense, and with some guidelines, you can greatly reduce the odds of being targeted for attack by someone you're dating or a new acquaintance.

- If a man asks for your phone number, don't reveal your home number right away. Give a work phone first. Or ask to call him. Try to get some information about him before you plan to meet—where he works, something about his life—so that if anything happens you have something to go on.

- Don't say too much too soon. Don't be specific about where you live (and with whom) until you feel safe. Don't be rude, but be aware of how much personal information you are revealing.

- On a first date, meet at a public place. Take your own transportation, or have enough money to get home.

- Alcohol plays a part in a huge percentage of acquaintance rapes. Be extra aware of your intake when you are nervous and in unfamiliar territory.

- Make sure someone else knows where you are and with whom.

- If you have a feeling that something is not right, excuse yourself and leave. Your life is precious and short, and you needn't spend time with someone who makes you uncomfortable. A person who respects you will understand later. Try not to make excuses. We are trained to be polite, and putting ourselves first can be difficult. Each time you respect your own feelings, your confidence will increase, and you will be less likely to be targeted for any type of crime. If you leave, make sure you are not being followed.

- If you are in a car and feel like you are being driven to a house or location against your will, be creative. Ask to stop to use the bathroom or to get food. Once out of the car, get help immediately and ask someone to call the police.

- Don't leave a party or other social situation with someone you've just met or don't know well.

- If you don't want to date or continue seeing someone, be clear and firm about ending the relationship. Be explicit. People often hear only what they want to hear when they have an emotional attachment. Don't negotiate. After you have stated your wishes, end the conversation. Rejections can be firm without belittling the other person. Saying "I'm sorry you feel differently. This is how I need things to be" should work.

Domestic Violence and Battering

Domestic violence, battering, spouse abuse: These are the names for the violence that happens in the home between two people who are, or have been, in a relationship with each other. The statistics are scary. Domestic violence is the leading cause of injury to women in the United States. Each day four women are killed as a result of battering. Nearly one-third of the women murdered in this country were killed by their husbands, boyfriends, or ex-partners. According to the American Medical Association, the "American home is more dangerous to women than the city streets."

Domestic violence can include physical, mental, or emotional abuse. Intimidating actions—punching walls, making verbal threats, or forcibly isolating a partner or spouse—are violent behaviors used to frighten and/or prevent a woman from doing what she wants to do.

Leaving a battering relationship can be extremely difficult and may take time, especially if there are children and financial commitments binding the victim to the batterer. Women need help—both concrete and emotional—to make the break. Call your local rape crisis center or the National Victim Center (800-FYI-CALL) for resources in your area. *Getting Free* by Ginny NiCarthy is a valuable self-help book for women trying to leave destructive or violent relationships (see Resources). Remember: Assault, even by family members, is a crime.

SIGNS OF A POTENTIAL BATTERER

Although men are most often batterers, both women and men can be abusive. Domestic violence is a problem in both heterosexual and homosexual relationships. Most batterers have a history of violence. Listen for clues about past relationships.

Are you in an abusive relationship? Physical abuse may take a variety of forms. Has your partner or an intimate done any of the following:

- Slapped, hit, pushed, or shoved you?

- Hit you with a fist? Kicked you?

- Hit walls? Thrown things at you? Destroyed property?

- Choked or raped you?

- Used a weapon against you? Threatened you with a weapon?

Emotional abuse may not be as easy to pinpoint as physical abuse. Check this list:

- Is your partner overly jealous?

- Do you find yourself lying about your whereabouts or activities even when you haven't been doing anything "wrong"? Do you live in fear of making him or her mad?

- Is he or she unable to deal with anger?

- Does he or she verbally threaten you with violence (even if he or she claims it would never escalate to actual physical violence)?

- Have you developed a cycle of violence and making up in which you become closer and/or engage in sex after a violent or angry outburst?

- Are you forced to have sex against your will?

- Are your children threatened?

Emotional abuse most often leads to physical abuse. If you answered yes to some of these questions, you may want to evaluate your options and plan a strategy for leaving this relationship. Domestic violence is one of the leading causes of death for women in this country. Get help. Check your phone book for listings under domestic violence, women's centers, or community services. You can also call (800) FYI-CALL for information about shelters and programs in your area.

Many battered women's programs offer free counseling to people in abusive relationships. Some provide counseling for batterers and for children living in violent homes. Most programs keep their information and records confidential.

Don't ignore dangerous behavior. If you are in an abusive relationship, plan ahead. Have money and important papers in a place where you can get them quickly should you have to leave in the midst of a crisis. And talk to someone—a friend, neighbor, or domestic violence counselor.

Dealing with Battering in the Community

If a woman you know is being abused, first let her know you care about her. Listen to her stories and let her know you will help. Do not judge or criticize her. Leaving a violent or abusive relationship is extremely difficult, and your relative or friend needs support. It takes women an average of seven attempts to leave an abusive relationship. Being supportive means committing yourself to helping through what may be a very long process.

- Find out what resources are in your area and encourage your friend to contact a shelter or program. Educate yourself about domestic violence and gather resources for your friend.

- Intervention may be possible if you are witness to an attack. Don't get physically involved yourself. If you are witness to violence or the threat of violence, call the police immediately. Don't underestimate the severity of the situation. Don't tell the police that someone is only being pushed around, or that it happens all the time. Tell them a life is being threatened—you want the police to respond quickly.

- Calling the police may save your friend from being injured or worse. The fact that someone has been called may stop the batterer from continuing. In many states, the police are required to press charges against a batterer even if the woman doesn't want to, or if she first decides to but later changes her mind.

On the street or in your neighborhood:

- Don't put yourself between a batterer and the victim—you are likely to be hurt.

- Don't ask a woman in an abusive relationship if she needs help. She is likely to say no, and if she says yes, she may be punished later. Instead, research what services are available in your area; write this information on a card and slip it secretly to the victim. Be as nonjudgmental as possible. You might say, "Someone in our building (or neighborhood) is being abused. If you know who it is, you might give her this information." Don't contact an agency directly on someone else's behalf; this invades the victim's privacy and most likely will be resented.

- If there is the immediate threat of bodily harm—a gun is pulled, the woman is down or bleeding—yell, "I'm calling the police," and go to get help. You might scare the abuser into stopping.

- If you have neighbors who fight violently, don't ignore it. Call the police and report screaming and fighting immediately. Your peace is being disturbed, and you may save someone from violent injury or even death.

- Call the police even if you are told not to get involved or that what happens in someone's home is none of your business. Tell the police not to reveal your name to the victim or the abuser so that you won't put yourself in danger.

- Don't offer your home as a shelter without considering the consequences of your offer. You may be putting yourself in danger, and your home probably won't provide the kind of distance the victim needs.

Stalking

Stalking is defined as willful, malicious, and repeated following or harassing of another person, and it usually begins with an obsession. Often, stalkers are former lovers or husbands, but they may also be strangers. Many states have passed antistalking legislation, which makes it a crime to engage in a pattern of behavior that harasses and/or threatens another person. Most laws require a threat of violence for the laws to be enforced.

Stalkers should not be ignored. A pattern of obsessive phone calls or letters can and often does escalate to violence. (See "Telephone Safety" in chapter 1 for what to do about harassment on the phone.) If you feel you are being stalked:

- Tell the police immediately. Be aggressive in getting the police involved. Provide a picture if possible. Keep a list of everything that happens—phone calls, threats, sightings—and file everything with the police. Save letters or notes received. A record is very important should you end up in court.

- Contact a domestic violence center for support. Call (800) FYI-CALL to find the center nearest you.

- Do not confront the stalker one on one. You will not change the person's behavior with rational argument and will only put yourself in danger.

- Tell friends, family, neighbors, and co-workers that someone is harassing you. Tell *everybody* not to give out personal information about you or your activities. Give people a description of the person stalking you. It's important for people to be aware of a potentially violent situation. If you work with the public, arrange with other employees for *you* not to have to deal with the harasser. House staff should be briefed on security precautions. Make sure house employees know not to discuss your life with anyone. If you live in an apartment with a manager or a guard, provide them with a description and photo if possible.

- Limit the amount of information available about you. Voter registration and driver's licenses can lead someone to your home. Use a post box for all mail and legal forms. Renting a private box is safer than using the U.S. post office. Change your mailing address at the DMV, and send notices to all businesses asking that they remove your street address from their files. Ask your friends to guard information about your address.

- Vary the routes you drive or walk to work or school.

- Do not accept packages unless you have personally ordered something.

- Consider legal means. A restraining order will require the stalker to stay away and stop the harassment, but these orders are difficult to enforce. Has the stalker broken any laws? Talk to the police about your options, or contact the clerk of your local court. Remember, a restraining, protective, or stay-away order is no guarantee of safety; it can only be enforced if broken, and it is often limited to a geographic area.

- You may want to keep a packed suitcase in your car, and extra cash, in case you have to make a quick escape.

- Arrange for a safe place to go to in case of emergency. Make sure the location or friend is unknown to the stalker.

If someone is stalking you, remember: You have done nothing wrong. The stalker is the one in the wrong. Being stalked is a terrifying, stressful, and emotional situation. You need support.

Campus Safety

A recent survey showed that one out of four college women have survived a rape or rape attempt. Nearly 85 percent of these women knew their attackers. Read and study the information about general self-defense and date rape. Date rape is the most common campus crime.

You have the right to question any stranger in your residence hall. "May I help you?" or "Who are you here to see?" will let the person know you are aware of his or her presence. If the stranger has no explanation for being there or seems nervous, get help: call either other dorm mates, the resident assistant, or campus security immediately.

More specific tips for campus safety:

- Do not post information on your whereabouts on your dorm room door.

- If you find a residence door that is propped open, close it.

- Lock your dorm room door, even if leaving for only a few minutes.

- If you study in out-of-the-way places during "off hours"—offices, labs, isolated parts of the campus—lock all the doors. If you still feel uncomfortable, tell the campus police where you will be working.

- Get together with a first-time date or study partner in a public place.

- Trust yourself and your instincts. If someone makes you feel uncomfortable, take action, even if you think you might be overreacting or behaving rudely.

- Find out if your campus has an escort service (male volunteers or campus police who walk female students to and from campus buildings after dark). Familiarize yourself with the escorts and the program before using it.

The National Victim Center provides a "College Security Questionnaire for Parents and Students" that you can ask campus police departments to fill out. The form requests campus crime statistics—for rape, assault, burglary, and drug violations—as well as specific information about security services at your college or prospective college. Call (800) FYI-CALL and ask for an information packet on campus crime.

SAFETY FOR CHILDREN AND TEENS

KIDS PICK UP ON AN adult's fears. In talking with your children about self-defense, try to keep your own fears from surfacing, however justified they may be. Listen to your child's concerns, and help them distinguish between unrealistic fears and justified dangers. Even by the age of three or four, kids have seen gory images on television (even in cartoons) and usually have developed some fears of their own. Children need to know you care about them enough to protect them. Both boys and girls should be instructed in self-defense and safety skills. As kids get older, don't be tempted to let down your guard, as most parents tend to do. Children from ten to eighteen are the most victimized age group.

Homework for Parents

- Carry current pictures of your children in your wallet and in your car. If anything should happen, you will be able to circulate a description immediately.

- Don't hang a house key around your child's neck: it's a sure sign to others that the child will be home alone.

- Name tags or marked clothing give an attacker the ability to call your child by name, creating false familiarity. Never mark the outside of belongings or clothes with your child's name. If you are asked to mark your child's clothes or belongings, do it discreetly so that a passer-by wouldn't be able to identify the name.

- Never leave your children unattended in a car. If you need to rendezvous with kids at a mall or theater, pick them up on the sidewalk or at a populated place; never meet them at the car. Parking lots are common venues for abductions.

Self-defense Basics for Children Ages Four to Twelve

When you explain safety rules, avoid detailing scary situations. Scaring your child into safe practices will not make him or her strong and confident, which is essential for effective self-defense. Confidence will help them appear less vulnerable, making them less likely to be targeted for attack.

AT HOME

- Leave your home address next to the phone so that in an emergency children can tell 911 where they live.

- Make concrete rules for opening the door: Never to strangers. Decide together who is okay.

- Outline safe phone use. Kids should never say their parents aren't home. Teach them to say, "I'm sorry, my mother can't come to the phone now. Who is calling?"

ACQUAINTANCES AND STRANGERS

Children have good instincts. Listen to your child's responses to strangers, family, and friends. If the child has a fear of someone or finds someone "creepy," validate those feelings and pay attention to the situation. Encourage kids to trust their gut feelings. Never belittle or disagree with a child's assessment.

- Most kids are victimized by people they know. Discourage the concept of the "scary man." An abductor can be a man or a woman, dressed stylishly or casually. The person might be a doctor, priest, or neighbor. An abductor might try to lure your children with candy or ask for help finding a lost kitten. An abductor may be a "friendly" man offering to pay for help washing a car or a "nice" woman claiming she is helping because Mommy was in an accident.

- Never instruct children to kiss or hug anyone. Allow them to decide what feels right. Teach children they have a right to say "no" to strangers and acquaintances. No one should touch them in ways that make them uncomfortable.

- Teach small children about privacy. Tell them it is illegal for any adult to touch their "private parts," even during "games." Explain that private parts are covered by bathing suits. Talk about the exceptions to this rule: supervised visits to the doctor and bath time for small children. Talk about secrets. No adult should expect a child to keep secrets from his or her parents or loved ones. Kids should be warned about "secret games."

- Act out situations. Role-playing can be fun for kids and adults. If your child is in a play group or preschool, suggest a safety skills workshop for the group. Make sure the teacher is experienced with children. Otherwise, brainstorm with other parents and teachers and use one another as "bad guys." Keep the play light but serious, and encourage the shiest kids to participate. If you project the attitude that self-defense is fun, children will pick up on it.

VERBAL AND PHYSICAL DEFENSE

- Teaching children to run from an attacker is fine, but they may run to an equally dangerous situation. Make sure your kids know who will really help them—running to "any adult" is not wise advice. Neither is running home if there is no parent there. Figure out "safe houses" in your neighborhood, on your child's route to school, and near other frequented places.

- Encourage children to speak up. Yelling and drawing attention to themselves is a positive reaction to danger. Yelling "Help!" does not always work—people think it's just kids playing. Instead, teach "Help! Fire!

Help!" Explain that people are afraid of fire and will quickly come to the rescue.

- Verbal self-defense for kids is much the same as for adults. "No. Stop. Leave me alone" is most effective. Some children will try "I don't know you." Discourage this response. Attackers and abductors often try to convince children they know them. A child should try to stop a stranger from approaching any closer than three feet. When practicing verbal responses, make sure the "Stop! No!" command comes as soon as the approach begins, not when the attacker is within range of picking up the child. If a child is being abducted, they should yell "Help!" and, if needed, "He's not my father!" or "She's not my mother!"

- Self-defense can also be used in peer situations. If a child is being bullied or harassed, responding with strong verbal defense is to be encouraged. "Stop. Leave me alone." This develops self-esteem and self-confidence.

- Teach about gun safety from an early age: Stay away from people with guns, even older kids with guns. Talk about gun violence—on TV and in the news. More children have died in the last twenty years from accidental gun shot wounds than did soldiers in the Vietnam War.

- Techniques for physical self-defense vary according to age and size. Hitting and making noise are effective for drawing attention. Other specific, simple techniques are kicking the shins, stomping the instep, and any strike to the throat (see chapter 7, "Physical Self-defense").

No! Go! Yell! Tell!

The four basic steps for children's self-defense are:

1. Say, "*NO!*"

2. *Go!* Run away!

3. *Yell* loudly, "Help! Fire! Help!"

4. *Tell* a parent or someone you trust what happened and describe who bothered you.

Teenagers and Safety

Teens should be taught basic street safety and self-defense skills. In addition, these issues should be discussed in the home or with trusted adults:

- Gun safety: No one should be carrying loaded or unloaded guns. Tell a trusted adult about any dangerous situation, even if you are told not to tell. If you are scared to tell, do so anonymously—write a letter or note and mail or deliver it to someone who will deal with the situation.

- Violence in teen relationships is now a big issue. Girls should not tolerate abusive behavior. Boys hit their girlfriends to control them, not because the girl has done something wrong. Parents should try to help their daughter—not shame or condemn her for breaking house rules or for going with the "wrong" boy. Supportive listening and helpful suggestions for getting out of the relationship will help develop a young woman's self-esteem, which is crucial for her choosing healthy relationships in the future.

- Teach teens to leave potentially violent situations— parties, crime sites, schoolyard fights. These days, a simple street fight can involve weapons and be potentially life threatening. "Don't be there" is the best advice.

- Teach teens to choose their group of friends wisely. Just because their friends are doing something doesn't mean *they* have to.

CHAPTER

7

PHYSICAL
SELF-DEFENSE

IN ORDER TO FIGHT BACK EFFECTIVELY you must value yourself enough to fight for yourself—*you must believe you are worth defending.*

Fighting back is a personal choice, and it depends on the situation. With a little training and a lot of conviction, everyone—of all abilities and sizes—*can* effectively resist attack. Of course, any choice of action you take while under attack is the right choice for you at that time. You may choose to resist, submit, or negotiate. Realistically, not every act of resistance will thwart every attack. To use the information in this book most effectively, you must prepare yourself and develop options that feel good to you.

Confidence and conviction are the most important factors in fighting back effectively. Confidence comes from being prepared. Prepare yourself mentally, and practice what you learn. Criminals won't expect you to fight back, and statistics show that fighting back—especially in rape attempts—will increase your odds of escape.

Self-defense is about choices. In each situation you are faced with many options—run? fight? submit?—and you must make your decisions quickly. This section will describe some of your options when facing various attacks and offer strategies for different situations. But each situation can be responded to in various ways; in every case you must decide for yourself what is the best action for *you*.

If you are faced with an attack, the most important thing you can do is think positively. This will keep your strength up. If your mind starts reciting negative thoughts—"I'll die here" or "I'll never get away"—breathe deeply. If you choose to fight back physically, pick your targets and strike with full conviction.

Read this section carefully and think about your options. Ask yourself questions. Visualize scenarios. Try to imagine yourself using these strikes. Practice what you learn. While you practice, combine these physical techniques with verbal and nonverbal defense. As difficult as it may be, thinking about these scenarios will help you to act if you should be attacked. *The most important thing is that you survive the attack.*

Practice these techniques. A close friend or relative might be a suitable practice partner, but be certain you pick someone you trust and who is wholly committed to seeing you succeed. Do not practice with someone who will criticize or dissuade you from learning. Remember, learning self-defense is a process, and you need to practice these techniques more than once. The physical self-defense in this book is designed to be simple, effective, and accessible to everyone, but it is not meant to be a substitute for a sound self-defense course. People with physical disabilities should adapt these techniques or omit those that are not feasible.

Not Being There: Running from an Attack

In the face of a physical attack, immediate retreat is an excellent option. Assess your situation: Do you have a clear path and a safe place to go?

Making a Scene: Attacks in Public Places

- Don't believe the attacker. If you are attacked in a public area and are told, "Don't scream or I'll shoot!"—*scream!*

- Yell, "Help! Fire! Help!" or "I'm being attacked, call the police! Call 911!" It has been shown that yelling only "Help" will not bring assistance as readily as "Help! Fire!" People respond to "Fire!" especially in crowded buildings or public spaces. If people are watching, tell them to call the police. They may be paralyzed with fear or not realize the severity of the situation.

- Throwing an object through a window might bring help and possibly scare off an attacker, especially if the attack is in a public but not very busy place, such as a back street or alleyway—or if the attack happens at night. Throw a rock, brick, briefcase, or purse, and throw *hard*. Assault against private property will usually cause either an alarm to sound, the police to come, or people to gather. Remember, a three-hundred-dollar plate-glass window is replaceable—your life is not.

Distracting Strategies

Some people have successfully thwarted attacks by acting crazy, urinating, or throwing up. You must, however, be fully committed to your plan so that you are convincing. On some occasions these strategies do work, but you must be very clear and not waver. Trust your gut feelings. If such a strategy seems right to you at the time, follow your instincts. However, these distracting strategies may also backfire and create an even more volatile situation, so you must fully commit to your plan.

When Should I Fight Back?

Each self-defense situation calls for assessment. Property and money are never worth fighting for; your safety is more important than material goods. If you are being held up for money, it is best to turn over your valuables and leave with your life. In more complex situations, you must assess various factors: Is there a weapon involved? What is the mental state of the attacker? How close are you to help? Answering these questions will give you a better view of your choices.

Don't get into a car with an attacker even if you are told you won't be hurt if you comply. Consider the source: Can this person be trusted? Getting into a car with an attacker lessens your chances of getting away without serious injury. If you are close to help, run and call for help as soon as you are able. Statistics show that going to a "secondary crime site" *drastically* increases your chances of being seriously injured.

Use Your Fear

Fear will send you a shot of adrenaline—use it to fight or flee.

- Breathe and tell yourself positive statements: I will be okay, I can find a way out of this.

- Don't be nice: You are being attacked. You have to hurt someone or get away to keep yourself safe.

- Don't cry or plead. Attacks and rapes are about intimidation; do everything you can to feel strong—even though you may feel nauseated, shaky, faint, or sick.

- Negotiation may be an option. Once you find out the intent of your attacker, you may be able to talk the person out of the attack or negotiate a compromise. Remember: Survival is your goal. You may have to comply with something the attacker asks to survive the attack. Trust your instincts, and remember, you are doing the best you can in a very scary situation.

The Self-defense Stance

When faced with a potential threat the most important thing is to appear confident and strong. When facing off with a potential attacker:

- Set your body at a 45-degree angle and keep your knees slightly bent. This stance protects your vital organs as well as gives you more mobility in case you need to move and run.

- Keep you hands toward the front of your body, below your waist. If you bring your hands up around your face, you might anger or threaten the attacker, causing the person to attack or grab them.

- Try not to back up—you don't know what or who might be behind you—and try not to fidget.

- Breathe deeply, feel your feet on the ground, and appear confident and strong.

- Use your nonverbal defense. Put on your "Don't mess with me" look (see page 35).

A TWO-ARMS' DISTANCE

Maintain a two-arms' distance between you and an attacker or harasser at all times. Stop someone with your voice before the person gets too close. "Stop! Step back."

When passing someone on the street who looks like a potential threat, glance back over your shoulder to make sure the person is not too close or following you.

Verbal Self-defense

Most attacks are preceded by some verbal exchange. A stranger will want to know if you are easily approached or intimidated. A huge percentage of self-defense situations can be stopped with nonverbal and verbal self-defense.

- If someone is coming toward you with aggression or ill-intent, yell, "No!" or "Stop!" This may well deter further action. One woman who was being held up at knifepoint told her attacker, "No! I can't go with you. I have to go to work." She was calm and firm, and this held him off until a car came by and she could signal for help.

- Take your self-defense stance, and follow up "No!" and "Stop!" with a command. "Leave me alone," or "Step back." Or, "I don't want to talk with you." Repeat the command. "Stop, step back. Leave me alone." Drunk or drugged people need repetition. Be specific. "Take two steps back. Do it *now*."

- Keep your voice low and even. Try not to sound panicky or scared—even if you are. Lowering your voice will help you sound confident.

- Do not engage in conversation. If you ask, "What are you doing?" you will probably be answered, "Nothing." Do not answer questions like "What's your problem?" Do not try to justify your actions. Simply repeat your commands over and over.

A typical response to a hostile man might sound like this: "Stop, get back. Leave me alone. Get back. Now. Step back. Do it now."

De-escalating Angry or Volatile People

You never know when a seemingly harmless situation may turn violent. De-escalating angry or volatile people is the safest way of dealing with what may be a potentially dangerous situation. You never know when a person may suddenly attack or reveal a weapon.

- Use strong verbal self-defense.

- In order to bring down someone's anger, you must speak firmly but do not shout. Let the other person know you are listening. "I understand you are angry. Calm down and I'll help you." "Calm down" or "Calm down and we'll talk about it" are phrases that signify active listening if you need to talk with the person who is angry.

- If the angry person is yelling, you must raise your voice but only to the level of the other person. Do not try to out-shout the person. Keep your voice calm, speak in a low tone, but increase your volume. Mirror the angry person's loudness while trying to keep the situation calm and controlled.

- Do not argue or use threatening gestures such as finger pointing or arm waving.

- Do not make threats or attack a person's behavior, telling the person to stop "acting stupid" or "being hysterical." This will escalate the confrontation. Swearing will also escalate the aggression level.

- Invite the person to sit down. Besides helping the person's body to calm down, this will give you the advantage should you need to leave quickly or fight back.

ANGER IN INTIMATE RELATIONSHIPS

Always remember that an angry person cannot listen to reason, and your safety comes first. What is the history of this person when he or she is angry: Does the person tend to calm down when spoken to? Or does the person continue to vent as long as there is an audience?

If you think the person will calm down, try stating assertively, "Calm down. Calm down, and we'll talk about this." Watch the response. Is the person getting more angry or settling down? If you choose this kind of de-escalation, make sure you know your options for escape.

If you fear for your safety, trust your gut feelings. Take space. Leave. Leaving might trigger more anger, so you may choose to offer a solution first: "Let's talk about this later." If the person needs specifics, set up a time and place, or suggest that a phone conversation take place either that evening or the next day.

When You Choose to Fight: Vulnerable Targets

When, by choice or necessity, you must fend off or fight with an attacker, you should have a clear idea of the best ways to strike. People usually think of the groin and the eyes as the most vulnerable areas of the body. Although vulnerable, they are also very difficult to strike. The groin is extremely difficult to target, and attackers know to keep themselves covered. And most people are too squeamish to poke the eyes with enough force to do damage. If you can do it, do it—jab or gouge—but don't do it halfway. You have to be fully committed.

For all attacks, remember: Keep striking and do not stop until either you have a clear escape route, your attacker retreats or is still, or help has arrived.

The Throat

The most vulnerable target on a person of any size is the throat. It takes eight pounds of pressure, about the force of hands clapping, to break a windpipe. Right now, take your fingers and press on your throat. Vary the pressure. Even the biggest, strongest man is built the same way you are. The throat is almost always an accessible target. (Heavy winter clothing may make the throat difficult to reach; however, a committed strike can be felt through several layers.)

THE Y-HAND STRIKE

Striking the throat can be done from close range or far away, even from within a bear hug. Make a Y with your thumb and forefinger. Thrust up and through the throat, aiming for the Adam's apple. This is an extremely effective strike that, when thrown with conviction, can stun, wind, or completely incapacitate an attacker. The Y-hand strike can be used from either a standing or a prone position, and even while sitting (for example, in a car).

- Make sure your fingers are fully extended, and you strike with the webbing between your thumb and fingers. Keep the webbing taut (Fig. 7.1).

- Strike through the target; do not stop when you make contact with the skin.

- For more power, start with your hand palm up on

Figure 7.1

your hip and rotate your palm downward as you strike with the Y-hand (Fig. 7.2). Use your body by rotating your hip to gain power.

- Speed will give you force. Throw the Y-hand as fast as you can.

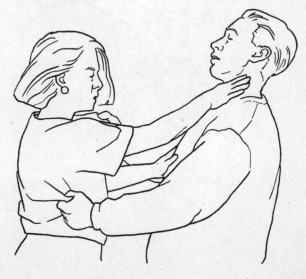

Figure 7.2

The Instep

A foot stomp is also an effective strike, and *the instep* is always an open target. Place your foot near the attacker's knee and stomp down, with force and speed. There are over two hundred tiny bones in the foot, and the hard ground does not provide much cushion on impact. Stomps can be done facing your attacker or if you are grabbed from behind (Fig. 7.3). Either way, a foot stomp is a good first reaction to a direct, close-in attack.

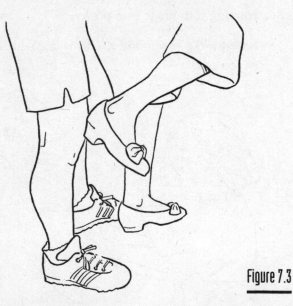

Figure 7.3

The Face and Head

The head, face, and temple areas are also important targets. A well-placed strike to the temple can knock out an attacker.

The *hammerfist* is an effective strike for the face or head. A strike that can be thrown from arm's length, a hammerfist will work from the front or side and is more powerful than a traditional punch.

- Make a fist and strike with the padded butt of the hand. Strike at a target such as the temple, nose, or throat (Fig. 7.4).

Figure 7.4

- A hammerfist can be thrown forward, as if you are throwing a ball or pounding a nail, or it can be thrown out to the side.

Yelling "No!"

Use your voice and yell "No!" with every strike. This is extremely important. Yelling will help you keep breathing through your fear, help you generate more power, and possibly attract attention. Weightlifters grunt for a reason when they lift weight: you gain an average of 17 percent more power in your strikes when you add the power of your voice.

Using Your Elbows

Most self-defense fighting and street fighting take place at close range, unlike in the movies where people exchange punches from two or three feet away. An attacker will most likely have you in a grip or bear hug or will be in body-to-body contact.

Landing a punch properly takes practice and skill, and punching won't work in most close-in fighting situations. Elbows are one of the best self-defense weapons, and anyone of any ability, size, and strength can use them. They are difficult to injure and hard enough to make good contact.

Basic elbows:

- Make a chicken wing with your elbow, folding your hand in toward your body and leaving the palm open and down. Bring your elbow across and back from the side of your body to the front, striking the face or throat (Fig. 7.5).

Figure 7.5

- Strike hard and fast. Speed will give you power.

- Strike with your elbow across your attacker's face, from temple to temple, and back again (Fig. 7.6).

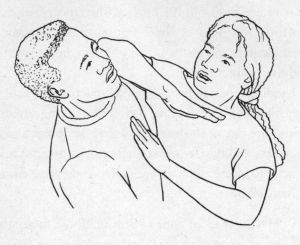

Figure 7.6

- Bring your elbow up under the throat and down onto the nose (Fig. 7.7). When you strike to the throat, bring your hand up as if you are brushing your hair back.

Practice throwing all four of these strikes in a row, quickly. These are ideal for striking someone who is very close, for instance, someone who has you in a bear hug.

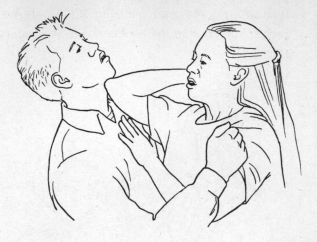

Figure 7.7

Remember: Follow up until you are free and can escape, your attacker is disabled, or help has arrived.

Situations for using elbow strikes:

- Bear holds, from the front or back. For a frontal attack, strike across the face. Strike over both shoulders, turning side to side if someone grabs you from behind. Try to strike up and over so you don't just hit the shoulders or arms. Aim for the head.

- On the ground. Elbow across the face as someone crawls in toward you. Elbow down into the groin if you find yourself on top of the attacker.

- If someone grabs you from behind. Elbow out over each shoulder or straight back next to your rib cage (Fig. 7.8).

Figure 7.8

- Being dragged by one arm. *Don't pull away, making the situation a struggle of strength.* Fold yourself toward the attacker and elbow across the face. Use the pull of the attacker for momentum (Fig. 7.9).

- Being choked from the front. Though not an elbow strike, a simple way to break a choke hold is to take an arm and punch over the attacker's arms toward the opposite wall (Fig. 7.10). If you use your right arm, raise it to shoulder height and punch directly

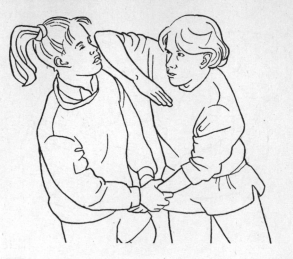

Figure 7.9

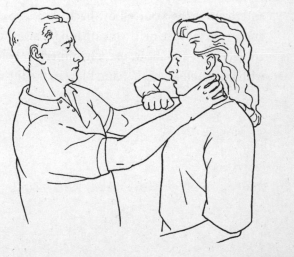

Figure 7.10

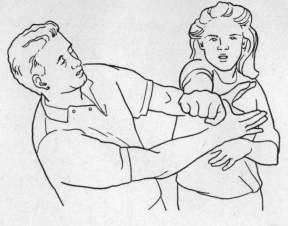

Figure 7.11

to your left—hard and fast (Fig. 7.11). You must follow through with your body, since turning slightly to the left will cause the attacker's hands to loosen and drop. Bring your elbow back across your body and strike the face or, if you are too far away to make contact with an elbow, use a hammerfist. Follow up with knees, elbows, a Y-hand blow to the throat.

Using Your Knees

Knees are better than kicks for close-in self-defense. You will keep your footing better on rough or slippery surfaces, and knees work from almost any position. Practice knees and elbows on soft couchbacks or pillows.

- Your knees should come up and down—almost like marching—but strike outward and think of hitting through your attacker (Fig. 7.12).

Figure 7.12

- Throw three or more knee strikes at once. The odds of landing a good strike multiply with repetition. You can use one knee up and down several times, or alternate your knees as if marching.

- Knees to the thighs and body really hurt when performed quickly with conviction. If you hit the groin, it's a bonus! Don't worry about the target, just bring your knees up and down, hard and fast. As you get space between yourself and the attacker you can follow up your knee strikes with an elbow or Y-hand blow to the throat.

- Shout "No!" while you knee: it will focus your energy and add power.

Kicking

Kicking to the shins may keep someone away, but you must be on firm, even, dry ground. Never kick above knee level, as you may lose your footing. A kick to the groin takes training and technique. If you are in close, better to use your knees or an elbow.

Using Your Head

If you are attacked from behind, tuck your chin in toward your chest, extend your head backward. Hit the throat or nose. Escape, or follow up this defense with elbow, knee, and Y-hand blows.

Zoning and Combinations

When striking, vary your targets: strike to the head, midsection, and knees and legs. This is called "zoning." If you strike only the head, even a not-so-smart streetfighter will block you after a few strikes. Instead, practice striking various targets. Throw an elbow to the head, follow with a knee to the body, and follow up with a kick to the shins or a stomp to the instep. An attacker who has been hit in the midsection will usually fold in the middle, which makes going to the head with a knee an obvious target.

Always throw three or more strikes when you are fighting back. Practice combinations, and never stop for assessment after throwing one strike. Your first strike might be deflected or not land squarely. Keep striking. Also, stopping affords an opportunity for your attacker to strike you. You must continue to fight until you have a clear path to safety.

Grappling and Struggling

Women will almost always lose a battle of power. Grappling will only tire you out. If you are grabbed, your choices have been taken away from you. Instead of struggling or wrestling, move in toward the attacker and strike, using an elbow, knee, hammerfist, or Y-hand blow. Moving toward the attacker is key, even though your first reaction will be to pull away. Pulling away puts you in a battle of strength.

For instance, if an attacker grabs both your wrists, free your hands by crossing them quickly across your body, right over left, and strike back with a hammerfist to the face. Speed is the key to this disarm. If the person has a good grip on your wrists and you can't break free, move in close and batter the body and legs with quick up-and-down movements of the knees. While the attacker is gripping your wrists, he is not able to further injure you.

Attackers are not prepared for a victim to move in. Scary as it seems, pulling away or grappling will escalate and prolong the attack.

The Option of Attacking First

If you know you are going to be attacked, you may choose to hit first. If someone has not responded to repeated verbal commands and still threatens violence, striking first may take your attacker off-guard. Make sure to take into consideration whether on not the attacker has a weapon.

- Step in with an elbow to a primary target such as the temple or throat. A Y-hand strike to the throat is a very effective first strike, as is a hammerfist.

- Throw knees and elbows to primary targets until your attacker stops and retreats or until you have a chance to escape.

- *Use your voice.* Shout "No!" while you strike. This gives you more power in your strikes, keeps you breathing, and calls attention to your situation.

Fighting from the Ground

Fighting from the ground gives great stability and power. Do not try to get up unless you are sure you can escape. (You may be grabbed from behind as you try to run.) Make sure your attacker is disabled before you get up from the ground.

If you are knocked down:

- Position your legs and feet facing the attacker.

- Lie on your side and use your hands for support. Kick out fast and hard, bringing your knees up to your body between strikes (Fig. 7.13).

Figure 7.13

- Target the knees (Fig. 7.14) and head (if the person is also on the ground).

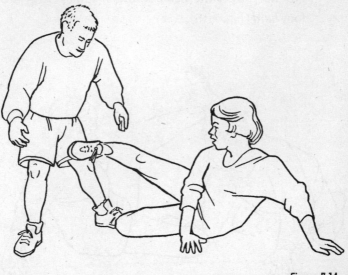

Figure 7.14

- If the attacker moves around you, shift your body from side to side and kick with the other leg. You can circle in this position by pulling yourself around and shuffling your legs. Practice this movement.

- An axe kick looks just like what its name implies. Bring your foot up and drop the heel straight down. This works well on attackers who are already on the ground. Target the head, kidneys, spine. Drop the foot *hard* (Fig. 7.15).

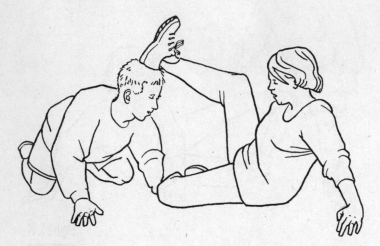

Figure 7.15

Using Walls or Buildings

- If you are pinned face forward against a wall, use the building for support. Turn your head sideways and place one hand under your face for protection (especially if your head is against the wall).

- Kick backward with your heel; stomp if the attacker is close.

- Use your elbows to jab back.

- If your back is to the wall, try to keep your spine and head from being hurt by leaning forward or shifting to your side so that your shoulder is against the wall. Use the wall for support.

- Use elbows if the attacker is close; kick low to the shins if the attacker is coming in.

- If the attacker lunges in at you, quickly turn to the side and push the person against the wall. Make sure you strike at a primary target before turning and running. Otherwise the attacker may grab you from behind.

Using Available Objects

Objects found in both house and garden can be used as weapons or for defense. Rocks, sticks, gardening tools, or fireplace implements can be used to strike effectively. You must fully commit and strike hard to a vulnerable target—such as the head—in order to disable an attacker. The danger of using available objects is that they can also be used against you. Make sure you use the implement as soon as you pick it up. Also, gardening tools that could be used as tools for entry or as weapons should not be left near doors or windows.

- Hot coffee, a purse, an umbrella, or a package can be thrown in the face of an attacker as a short distraction.

- A jacket can serve to "catch" a knife: with your hand on the shoulder and sleeve area, throw the jacket toward the knife as if you were throwing a net.

- If you cannot get away immediately, quickly follow up either action with elbows, knees, and other strikes.

Blocking and Protecting Yourself

Fancy karate blocks are learned over time, but you can protect your vital targets with simple protection moves.

- The self-defense stance: Always stand sideways when facing an attack in order to better block your vital targets.

- Blocking punches: Do not try to stop a punch with your hand. You must have energy and force in your arm to block a strong blow. Instead, throw your body toward the attacker so that you are close to *their* body and therefore not at the end of the strike. Get in very close—body to body. Then use knees and elbows.

- Blocking strikes to the head: Raise your hands in fists and place them tightly on either side of your head. Tuck your chin to your chest. Assess your situation: Can you strike back or escape?

- Keep moving. A moving target is harder to hit.

- If you are being kicked while on the ground, ball up and protect your head and neck with your hands. Your spine and kidneys are also vulnerable, so try to protect them as best you can. Roll next to a wall or a piece of furniture.

Facing Weapons

Statistics show that only one in four sexual assaults on women involve a gun or a knife, whereas most robberies involve a weapon. In addition, you don't always know if someone is carrying a concealed weapon that could be used.

Where weapons are involved, play it safe.

Guns are usually used for intimidation and control. If an attacker wants to shoot you, that can be done from a distance or when the person first approaches. A man wielding a gun wants something. *Ask him what he wants.*

"What do you want? I'll give you anything you want, just don't hurt me." This will give you time to figure out what is happening. Make sure you keep your eyes on the weapon and remind yourself to keep breathing.

- Hand over money or valuables.

- Act quickly if you think you can escape. Run. An attacker will usually not fire at an escaping victim.

- Fighting against an armed attacker is an option, but you have to be fully committed. If you figure this is your best option, try to find a moment when the attacker is off-guard or has dropped the weapon, then use whatever techniques are available (Y-hand, elbow, etc.) until you have disabled the attacker, gained control of the weapon, or have time to escape. If you gain possession of the weapon, *make sure you maintain distance* from the attacker and are ready to use the weapon or escape. You don't want the attacker to regain control of the weapon.

- Going along with the attack may be your best option, especially if you think this will save your life. During the attack, gather information about your attacker should you choose to report to the police. Due to emotional responses, or because in some areas the legal system is still rough on rape victims, not all survivors report their victimization. But most city or precinct police officers are trained to be sensitive to rape survivors, and in many places you will be assigned a female officer to guide you through the filing process. You can also have a friend, family member, or trained support counselor from a rape crisis center with you during the reporting.

More complicated gun and knife defenses are taught in advanced self-defense classes.

Special Situations

IN THE SHOWER

If you happen to be in the shower when someone attacks, there are several options. If you are not going to be attacked right there in the shower, get out as quickly as possible. This can give you time to figure out your options for escape, or for fighting back with a household weapon, or for talking your way into a different scenario. Once out of the tub, you will be better able to use your knees for defense without fear of slipping. If you can use the walls for support, you may want to knee and elbow right there in the shower. Try to maneuver so that you can escape.

If the shower is large—if it has a tub—you may want to drop to the ground. A struggle standing might get you banged up and hurt in a fall. On the ground, strike straight at the knee with an elbow to topple the attacker. You must follow up with a disabling blow, such as a Y-hand or strike to the throat or kick to the head.

Your goal is to get to safety. Even if you are unclothed, leave the house at once. Do not stop to grab clothing. Getting to help and safety is more important than temporary discomfort or embarrassment.

IN BED

If you wake up to find someone on top of you in bed, try not to panic: breathe deeply and try to calm your mind. Assess what, if any, weapons are present. Use this time to calm yourself and make a plan.

- The attacker will take time to move the covers and adjust his clothing. This is a good time to make a move, while he is distracted.

- If you are on your back, try not to let him get you fully pinned. Pull one knee up and arch your back so that you are not flat against the bed (Fig. 7.16).

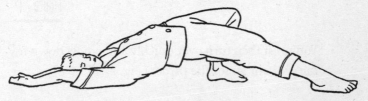

Figure 7.16

- While he is on top, or getting on top, strike to the back of his body with the knee of the extended leg (Fig. 7.17). Strike with the knee hard and fast and straight up toward your head as far as you can. This will topple the attacker back toward the head of the bed.

Figure 7.17

- You must then turn over quickly and elbow down to the groin or go for the throat (Fig. 7.18).

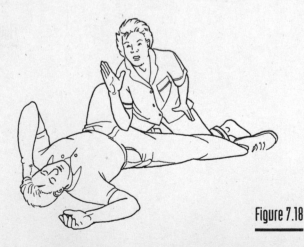

Figure 7.18

- Do not get up from the bed until you have disabled your attacker enough to escape. If you turn and run, he will probably grab you from behind.

A GROUP ATTACK

In a group attack, avoid being surrounded. Try to keep all the attackers together so that you have an escape route, should an opportunity arise. Think of situating yourself so that they are lined up.

If the attack has not begun, use your verbal skills to prevent the attack. Target either the weakest attacker—there is usually someone who is not fully committed to the crime—or the ringleader. Freely offer your wallet or purse. Assess how close help might be. Will screams for help be heard? Try not to show your fear. Observe the attackers for markings for later identification.

Mace, Tear Gas, and Pepper Spray

Mace, pepper spray, or tear gas can be effective—if they are used correctly. (Mace is a trademarked name for a specific brand of tear gas.) But most people who carry a spray aren't properly trained, practiced, or ready to use it at the moment of attack. Mace is a weapon, and if you plan to carry it, you *must* practice and be prepared—otherwise, as with all weapons, it may be taken and used against you.

These sprays work by irritating mucous membranes and respiratory systems. Pepper spray, made with a high concentration of capsicum (derived from hot peppers), is the most effective type of self-defense spray. The spray affects the eyes and respiratory system, usually works in seconds, and lasts up to a half hour. First the eyes will close, then the assailant will have trouble breathing, and there will be an intense burning in the throat.

Before purchasing or carrying a self-defense spray, check with police regarding state and local regulations regarding use. In many areas, you must be licensed and trained to carry a spray. In some states, carrying tear gas or pepper spray is illegal.

- For tear gas or pepper spray to be effective you must have it handy. You must practice pulling it out and know where the button is without looking at the device. In high-stress situations, you often lose manual dexterity. *You must be extremely familiar with your weapon.* A spray stored in a pocket or purse is useless at the time of an attack; you must be able to respond in seconds. You need to have your spray in hand at the time of attack.

- You must target the face for this spray to be effective. Even so, several recent studies show that persistent attackers will not stop their attack when hit by Mace. Most pepper sprays can fire up to ten feet, but it is best to fire when your attacker is about five feet away.

- You must be careful of the wind direction when spraying; you cannot walk in the mist or you yourself will be affected. You cannot spray in a confined area, like a car or small room. You must be able to leave the site immediately.

WARNINGS ABOUT SPRAYS

- Pepper spray does not work on everybody; about 20 percent of the population will not respond adversely to the capsicum.

- Chemical weapons expire and are useless after their expiration date. Extreme weather changes affect them.

- Don't take sprays through airport checks; you will be stopped and questioned.

- *Do not let carrying a self-defense spray lull you into a false sense of safety.* Carrying a spray for peace of mind will only trip you up in the end.

Stun Guns

Stun guns do not look like regular guns. They are T-shaped, with a pronged tip. This tip delivers a jolt that affects the attacker's nervous system. In order for these weapons to be effective, you must be close enough to the attacker to make physical contact, and you must be able to hold the gun in place for nearly two seconds. The attacker is not knocked out cold, but he or she will be incapacitated. Depending on the gun and the strength of the jolt, the effect may wear off in minutes. There are no long-term effects. These guns are not recommended for anyone who is not trained in self-defense and weaponry, and they are illegal in many states.

The market is being flooded with new personal safety devices. A dart gun that shoots electrically charged barbed probes can hit an attacker fifteen feet away, but you must have the gun ready and be a good shot. The jolts affect neuromuscular control, but do no lasting damage. You must also be able to follow up with self-defense, or get away. These devices are difficult to obtain, need to be registered, and are illegal in many states.

Be wary of new gimmicks in security devices. Remember that any hand-held device must be readied and aimed accurately at the precise moment of attack to be effective.

Owning or Carrying a Gun or Other Weapon

Having a gun in your home makes it three times more likely that someone will be killed there—and this someone is usually a child. More than fifty thousand children have been killed in the United States by firearms since 1979. Having a gun in the house is a dangerous proposition, especially if you have children living or visiting there.

There are several ways to store a gun safely—break it down and hide the bullets elsewhere, place it in a special safe box, or attach a locking device to the trigger—but, of course, these make the gun difficult to use in an emergency. If you do not have children in your home, you will have to assess where the gun is handy and most safe.

Owning a gun is an individual decision. If you face an attacker with a gun, you must *be practiced* and be prepared to use it. You might choose to wound or maim, rather than kill, but you should practice on a target and be prepared to fire the weapon.

Don't own a gun if you are ambivalent about using it. You have to know in your mind that you will shoot a weapon before you pick it up; otherwise an attacker will read your fear. If you shoot someone in justifiable self-defense, you will not be prosecuted. However, there are women in prison today who shot their abusive partners and were found guilty of murder because they were not defending themselves at the precise moment of the shooting.

If you choose to own a gun, take a gun safety and handling course.

Witnessing an Attack

If you are witness to an attack, it is best not to get physically involved. Getting involved often means you will be hurt or victimized.

If you are with someone who is attacked, but you are not, it is best that you go for help. Do not stay and fight—especially if there are weapons involved. This is most difficult when you must leave behind someone you love deeply, such as a child, partner, or friend. However, it is important that both of you do not get injured or abducted. If you stay, this might happen.

- Yell "I'm calling the police."

- Run and get help immediately. Call the police. The attacker may worry about your whereabouts and the possibility of help or the police arriving and may abandon the attack.

- Try to remember details of the attack and descriptions of those involved. This will help the police.

- Teach this to children as well. If two children are approached, and one child is grabbed, the other should immediately go for help.

Self-defense Classes

In addition to giving you practical, preventive, and easy self-defense moves, a good self-defense course will make you feel more powerful, increase your self-esteem, and give you more options and freedom in your life. Those who have been victims of assault or abuse may find that a supportive course helps them work through fear, anger, or self-blame.

If you want to try a self-defense course in your area, be sure to check out the program and instructors before you sign up. Every karate center in the country advertises self-defense training, but most karate schools teach complicated and difficult techniques that are not street safe and take years to perfect. Here are some questions to consider when choosing a course, either for yourself or your children:

- What are the credentials of the instructor? How long has he or she been teaching? Does the instructor make you feel comfortable and safe?

- Always view a class before signing up. Are all the students respected and encouraged?

- Does the course take place over a manageable period of time? Better to take a short course than to sign up for an extensive one and miss classes.

- Does the training include verbal, nonverbal, and physical training? Some martial arts–oriented courses bypass verbal training. Verbal self-defense is absolutely crucial and is the foundation for other training. Never take a self-defense course that doesn't emphasize verbal skills.

- Are the physical defenses easy and safe? Self-defense moves are basic (knee and elbow strikes, hammerfist blows) and can be learned by people of all ages and physical abilities. In viewing a course, note the success rate of students. Every student should be successful within a short period of practice.

Some of the best courses use a padded attacker, for both the verbal and physical training. Having to use all your self-defense skills against a "real-life" attacker helps push through fear and builds confidence. These courses can be expensive, but shop around. There are several types of padded-attacker programs now offered in most areas. Call your rape crisis center, gay and lesbian hotline, university women's center, or local YWCA for referrals.

RESOURCES

CRIME VICTIM ASSISTANCE PROGRAMS

Most large counties and some smaller ones have victim assistance programs geared toward helping victims of crime get justice or financial help. Locate the center nearest you through the police, a crisis center, or by calling the National Organization for Victim Assistance at (800) 879-6682. Most states have limited funding available for emergency medical care, lost wages, or rehabilitation. A victim assistance counselor might help you find counseling (short- or long-term depending on your needs); help you get emergency financial assistance; give information about support groups; and help you apply for long-term financial assistance.

To be eligible for state aid compensation, you must report the crime to the police within seventy-two hours, then file a claim by the state's deadline, usually a year later. The criminal need not even be identified for you to receive assistance.

ASSOCIATIONS

The National Victim Center Toll Free Information and Referral Service offers a toll-free information line with access to over five thousand victim assistance programs nationwide. INFOLINK is not a crisis or counseling line, but they will connect you with these services in your area. IN-FOLINK also provides information bulletins and resource packages on over sixty topics, including rape, robbery, assault, and stalking. You can call INFOLINK at (800) FYI-CALL (394-2255) from Monday through Friday from 8:30 A.M. to 5:30 P.M. Eastern Standard Time.

National Crime Prevention Council
1700 K Street NW, 2nd floor
Washington, DC 20006-3817
(202) 466-6272
FAX: (202) 296-1356

The National Crime Prevention Council produces a full range of materials and resources about safety, including an informative series for children called "Taking a Bite Out of Crime" that features a dog detective. *Are You Safe? A National Test on Crime Prevention* is an excellent video for individuals or community groups undertaking crime prevention education. Call for more information and a list of resources.

National Organization for Victim Assistance (NOVA)
1757 Park Road, NW
Washington, DC 20010
(800) TRY-NOVA (879-6682)
or (202) 232-6682

A private, nonprofit organization, NOVA provides information and referrals to victims of crime. Callers on the 24-hour, toll-free number will receive information about local victim assistance programs and services. Callers to the office number may also be able to speak with a crisis counselor during working hours (Monday through Friday from 9 A.M. to 5 P.M. Eastern Standard Time).

BOOKS OF INTEREST ON DOMESTIC VIOLENCE

Seal Press-Feminist publishes a series of practical, multicultural, easy-to-read books on the issue of violence against women. There are culturally sensitive books targeted toward Latina, Filipina, and African-American women. These books are specifically for women who want to identify physical, emotional, and sexual abuse and free themselves from it. See especially *Getting Free: You Can End Abuse and Take Back Your Life* by Ginny NiCarthy (1986) and *In Love and In Danger: A Teen's Guide to Breaking Free of Abusive Relationships* by Barrie Levy (1992). For additional titles, contact Seal Press-Feminist, 3131 Western Avenue, #410, Seattle, WA 98121 (206-283-7844) and inquire about the New Leaf Series.

STREETSMARTS WORKSHOPS

For information about Streetsmarts self-defense workshops, lectures, or seminars, contact Louise Rafkin, P.O. Box 1010, Truro, MA 02666 or leave a voicemail message at (508) 487–2456.

INDEX